Bitterbrush Country

Living on the Edge of the Land

Diane Josephy Peavey

Fulcrum Publishing
Golden, Colorado

Library of Congress Cataloging-in-Publication Data

Peavey, Diane Josephy.
  Bitterbrush country : living on the edge of the land / by Diane
Josephy Peavey.
      p. cm.
  ISBN 1-55591-293-1
  1. Idaho—Description and travel. 2. Idaho—Environmental conditions.
3. Idaho—Social life and customs. 4. Ranch life—Idaho. 5. Country
life—Idaho. 6. Natural history—Idaho. 7. Peavey, Diane Josephy. 8.
Women ranchers—Idaho—Biography. 9. West (U.S.)—Description and
travel. 10. West (U.S.)—Environmental conditions. I. Title.
  F750.P43 2001
  979.6'033—dc21
                                    2001002331

Printed in the United States of America
0 9 8 7 6 5 4 3 2 1

Editorial: Marlene Blessing, Lori D. Kranz, Daniel Forrest-Bank
Cover and interior design: Trina Stahl
Interior formatting: Cyndie Chandler
Cover painting: *Tree Grove & Road* (oil on canvas, 16" x 20"), copyright © 2001
    Ginna Parsons Lagergren.
Back cover photograph: View through the author's ranch house window. Photo by
    Diane Josephy Peavey.
Interior illustrations: Ginna Parsons Lagergren

Fulcrum Publishing
16100 Table Mountain Parkway, Suite 300
Golden, Colorado 80403
(800) 992-2908 • (303) 277-1623
www.fulcrum-books.com

*To John, who brought me home and shared with me
his love of the land and his stories*

*And to my parents, Alvin and Betty, who opened the world to me
and then encouraged my writing of its adventures*

Contents

Author's Note

I am deeply grateful to the staff and management of KBSU Idaho Public Radio for providing weekly airtime for my stories. It has allowed me to chronicle life in the West over the last decade. Many of the places and circumstances in these writings have changed since I first wrote about them. Please see these stories as moments in time and not representations of what is today. I thank the listeners of that radio station who have encouraged me and especially those who have told me their own stories, usually of family ranch operations several generations old that have been lost.

I thank my husband, John, who has inspired me to love this landscape and listen to its stories. Our son, Tom, his wife, Diane, and their sons, Cory and Jake, all of whom daily share the joy and hardships of this life with us. The matriarch of our family, Mary Brooks, whose father started Flat Top Sheep Company and who held the ranch together for her son and grandson. David Peavey and his family and Karey who support us from afar. Our sheep managers, Denny Burks, and his family and his father, Dennis, before him. Rod and Humberto, our head cowboys over the years, and now Rafael who takes over the job and Juan and all our sheep herders.

And finally my loving thanks to my editor and friend Marlene Blessing, who has made my journey from radio to printed page an inspiration.

As I write this, our region of the West is coping with the effects of record-low winter snows and anticipating a summer of severe drought, fire, and loss. Front-page stories in the newspaper warn of irrigation water for crops lasting 60 days this season, half of its normal supply. Despite green desert feed for our animals, we are already hauling water to them daily. It is reminiscent of the drought ten years ago. Yet, the sandhill cranes return, the sage hens are booming, and the bitterbrush fills the landscape with its fragrant yellow blossoms. Life changes and life repeats itself. We persevere.

Introduction

My home is the vast, open landscape of south-central Idaho, at once a sanctuary, a source of strength, and a heartache.

The land is in remote, breathtaking country of tall grasses, sagebrush, and basalt rock buttes that roll gently up and into the Pioneer Mountains, all framed by an endless stretch of sky. The smallest section of this landscape was tamed by my husband's family, who has raised sheep for three generations and Angus cattle since 1960. For years, it remained a refuge in its isolation.

This was not always my home and I came to it slowly, cautiously, an urban woman far more comfortable on freeways than dirt roads, more assured inspiring a staff than herding cows. For over ten years after I married, I performed a dance of courtship with this landscape, alternately pursuing then fleeing its demands.

In part my reluctance came from our uncertain future, faced as I was immediately by the farm crisis of the 1980s. I rejected intimacy with a place I might suddenly lose. Then there was my personal sense of inadequacy, my uncertainty that cowboying was my lot, something I still question in this man's environment. But now I have found my place here, without becoming cowgirl of the year, roping, riding, and castrating everything in sight. I am at home.

When I arrived in 1981, I was familiar with this country. Although I was raised an easterner, when I was a child my family traveled west each summer. My father was a writer and historian, and our trips zigzagged across western highways, from abandoned Anasazi villages in southern Colorado to the Blackfeet All-Indian Days in Browning, Montana. My father was always researching, moving from one piece of western history to another.

In between as we drove what seemed like endless hours through slow-changing landscape, he entertained us with the stories of the area to calm our restlessness. Suddenly, on the open Nebraska prairie, we could see Pawnee Indians making their way by horseback to the Platte River. In

Utah's red rock desert, we could make out Mormon pioneers lowering their wagons down steep cliffs as they moved west. Repeatedly our father turned boredom into adventure for the four children in the backseats of the station wagon.

On an early trip, we discovered the beautiful country of the Wallowa Valley in northeastern Oregon. The area had been the homeland of the famous Chief Joseph and his band of Nez Perce Indians, and my father was doing research for his book, *The Nez Perce Indians and the Opening of the Northwest.*

In this remote western country, our family built a house on a hill under the rugged peaks of the Wallowa Mountains, next to Silver Lake Creek, under full cottonwoods. Beginning in 1962, we would retreat to this spot each summer from our East Coast lives to fill our souls with the space, quiet, and the stories that spilled from the people and the landscape.

Here in this small ranching and mill town, things moved slowly and we learned the rhythms of rural America, dancing to cowboy music and slipping into the cadence of ranching stories told by family friends like the McClarens and the Tippetts, who had run livestock in this country for generations. As a young working woman, I continued to spend vacations in the Wallowas, returning to my urban apartment each year with huge plastic sacks filled with sagebrush, wild grasses, and flowers. These treasures were a reminder for me throughout the year of a landscape so intriguing, so compelling I could not leave it behind.

In the 1970s, I moved to Alaska, where I learned about remoteness, friendships, and community, and the ways each provided strength against the enormity of nature. I left the state to join a cadre of friends working on the Alaska Lands legislation in Washington, D.C. It proved to be a four-year, all-consuming commitment and when the bill was signed into law December 2, 1980, I planned my return to that northern state. On my way, I stopped in Idaho and met a rancher and state senator, John Peavey, the man I would later marry.

It was through John that my western education began in earnest. He was third-generation owner of a sheep and cattle operation, one of the largest ranches in the state. At our first meeting, we talked about the Sagebrush Rebellion. In 1980 when this movement was gaining strength throughout the region, I was a special assistant at the Department of the Interior in Washington. At agency meetings I listened to my colleagues translate the angry words of westerners who demanded that the federal government turn over management of public lands to the states. The struggle for control of this sprawling region intrigued me, although I was not a supporter of the rebellion.

Now I was surprised, and relieved, to find a livestock man who opposed the movement. But I soon learned John was unusual among his peers. He had resigned from the Idaho Cattleman's Association because of its partisan approach to land issues. He was a state senator, a Republican at first. Politics and the GOP were a family tradition. His grandfather and stepfather were both United States senators, and his mother was director of the U.S. Mint.

But John's issues were his own and he became a lightning rod, calling for a moratorium on new development projects draining the Snake River at an alarming rate, protesting nuclear weapons development and the lethal waste storage at the National Engineering Laboratory near farming communities and over the aquifer that provides water for southern Idaho. He led the effort on a statewide initiative for campaign and lobbying finance disclosure against the powerful corporate interests that preferred to operate in secrecy. These issues made him a maverick and soon an outsider in his party, and in 1980 he became a Democrat. He continued to win reelection to the state senate until he retired in 1994 to make a run for lieutenant governor.

In the beginning, it was a love of politics that brought us together. But soon I realized John was first of all a man of the land and that his politics led him to protect what he knew best and valued most.

Today we are a ranching family. John's mother, Mary Brooks, at ninety-three, spends the summers at her house beyond the ranch cook shack watching the birds outside her window, tending her flowers, and driving around the ranch to check on the progress of the crops and livestock. Unable to walk well these days, she nods her approval from the driver's seat of a car whose plates read "Mtn Mary."

My husband's youngest son, Tom, is thirty-six and runs the ranch with his father. Tom and his wife, Diane, have two boys, Cory and Jake, and I wonder if one of them will become the fifth generation to care for this place. My husband's two eldest children live away from the ranch. David, an engineer, with his wife, Arlynn, and three sons, Aaron, Adam, and Benjamin, live in California. His daughter, Karen, is a corporate accountant in Washington State.

John, unlike his family before him, expanded the ranch capacity, adding cattle to the sheep operation and absorbing the Jim Laidlaw ranch into the original Flat Top Sheep Company.

As for me, I continue to learn about this place from my husband, listening to his stories, watching him work the land and livestock, and sharing his connection to this place. But I have developed my own attachments slowly.

In the beginning, I was intrigued by the romance of this landscape. But that was before I became intimate with it, before the pain caught up to the joy, before I saw my own story merge with those around me.

In the 1980s, we, like so many other landowners, came close to losing our ranch. We whispered the word "bankruptcy," afraid of its sound and its hand on our future. Perhaps to subdue my own fears, I became the director of a small family farm organization, a group of farmers trying to help each other survive the depression, its foreclosure notices, and the confusion of dislocated lives.

While I worked for others, we struggled at home. Several years later, when I left the organization, I looked around me at our ranch with new eyes. I had faced the possibility of loss and fought back. Now I would write, hoping my words could save what the fickle marketplace might not.

At first my stories were random, inspired by unusual episodes, the small events of this ranch life. Like the day a bull roamed into the yard of our ranch cabin, no one around but me, and he only inches away from my window, hoof-deep in peonies. Then there was a story of the first meal I cooked for the cowboys on our cattle drive. Alone in the camp kitchen with nothing but miles of sagebrush desert around me, I swore at the lumps in the pot roast gravy as I wished for pasta, pesto, and running water.

I bundled up my first writings and took them to the closest public radio station in Boise, KBSU, three hours away from home. The staff liked my stories and gave them weekly airtime. Nine years later the stories continue.

I began to write in memory of friends who left the land, losing their balance in life. All of us struggled against huge economic odds and a marketplace run by multinational corporations that fixed prices far below the cost of production. Then came stories prompted by a new fear, as environmentalists (of which I am one) and cattlemen (of which I am one) shouted at each other over the very thing they shared in common: a love of the land. The strident voices were frightening—neighbors and friends at war with each other. Radical environmentalists made newspaper headlines, demanding that we be thrown off grazing lands we'd used for decades and depended upon for survival. As a lifelong environmentalist, I was stunned. As a rancher, I was terrified. Between extremes, I planted myself in the center, looking for solutions to save both the land and its people. In the midst of this acrimony, we could not hear the chatter of developers who stood on the sidelines, fueling our anger while they watched.

As John and I traveled the backroads and small towns of the West, we found stories in a landscape marked by broken dreams, abandoned cabins, and ghost towns, visible memories of the hard work and determination of people who tried but could not sustain themselves in this landscape. There were communities like Pahrump, Nevada; Grasmere, Idaho; the Mohave, Armagosa, and Harquahalla Valleys in Arizona and Nevada. And of these towns, the ones that survived have turned into recreational developments, a clutter of trailer parks, motels, and condominiums scattered across hillsides in a blaze of irrigated green lawns glued down over brown desert grasses.

The traditional keepers of the land are cleared away, bought out, and the landscape turns from quiet introspection to carnivalesque cacophony. And I am afraid we are losing our direction in the confusion and our souls in the reckless grab for the future.

Today, those of us on the land are battered by farm policies that urge us to "get big or get out," and we know that family farmers cannot keep up with corporate farming monopolies. But we cannot give up trying either. When we least expect it, the markets soar, making our crops and livestock valuable again. We breathe a sigh and allow ourselves to think about a new pickup or putting new flooring in the cabin kitchen. Then the erratic moods of weather, of droughts and early frosts, humble us again. It is a dizzying ride over which we have little control.

But we are determined to survive, because at its heart ours is the most primitive struggle—for home, for place, and for belonging. Often I find myself wanting little more than to retreat from the debate to this land where quiet brings resolve and work calms the panicked heart.

These stories are a personal journey of discovery and of wonder at the smallest details and the grandest landscapes offered up by this western country. It is a love story of sorts, a glimpse into why, despite political and economic odds that threaten everything we love, we stay. After years of reluctance, I am finally at home in this landscape. And I have learned one thing: the constant in the West and on our ranch is change.

So I find myself racing to capture its small pleasures and gifts, its memories, even as they slip away. In these stories, I do not try to tackle the almost cataclysmic social, economic, and political issues we face daily, although there are hints of them throughout these pages.

Instead this is a collection of moments and memories, the reasons I have stayed—fields of camas flowers, sandhill cranes, stories learned from old homesteaders, the quiet of a sunset, the comedy of my first attempts to vaccinate calves, all the stories I never knew until I found my way home.

Here, then, are sketches of our land, our life at Flat Top Sheep Company ranch and in the West I have come to know over the past nineteen years. Each piece is a detail, a mere snapshot. But taken together, the stories create a broad picture of this life and of a landscape that ignites the passions of so many. Perhaps none more than my own.

Prologue: Seasons

My life is defined by seasons on this remote sheep and cattle ranch. Here in the foothills of the Pioneer Mountains in south-central Idaho, the years pass, small routines vary, but the days play themselves out in the flow of seasons, filling in cycles of life and death, promise and pain.

It is like this. It was winter when we met, spring when we discovered our love, summer when we married, and fall when I realized the strong pull of this land on me.

I first glimpsed this vast ranch in winter with its owner from his Cessna 182 airplane. The fields were covered with snow. John pointed below to the 16 miles of fencing that enclosed the huge headquarter's meadow and hay fields. We flew up draws and over ridges where cattle and sheep roamed in summer. We skimmed over willows and naked cottonwood trees that lined creek banks. We circled over black cows eating from long green ribbons of hay looped across white fields of snow.

He told me theirs was a cow-calf operation, Black Angus cattle. Until that day, I thought that to be in the cattle business was to raise steers for beef. I never considered how they were bred or born, never questioned the cycles of life.

It was spring when my friend first drove me to his ranch, turning east off the highway from the Sun Valley resort community onto the 24-mile dirt road to his home. On that trip, we stopped at the summit 8 miles past the turnoff to stare into a vast expanse of space and quiet that both frightened and thrilled me. In late spring, I crossed the southern Idaho desert on horseback for the first time, herding cattle home to summer pastures.

It was summer when I raked cut hay before it was baled; summer when I heard, then saw, the sleek sandhill cranes strutting through alfalfa fields. It was my first summer at the ranch when I helped herd our sheep north through the early-morning quiet of the Ketchum resort community while its people slept. The animals would graze in isolated mountain pastures north of us. And a year later, it was summer when we were married in front of our ranch cabin. Flowers bloomed and the days were full of promise.

In fall the hunters came. We rounded up the cattle and sheep, ending their days of mountain grazing. It was fall when we decided to move our animals to warm pastures in other regions of the West, and fall when the trucks came to haul them south. The hillsides turned burnt orange, then red, then the silence came, followed by the snows and icy weather that forced us to move to town after draining pipes at the ranch and putting away summer things for another season.

It was that winter I knew I would stay with this man, on this land, connected to a life simple and complex at once. I had watched him care for the dogs and horses, move the sheep, run his hand through moist spring dirt, and pluck midsummer leaves from crops, then roll them in his palm to measure their readiness. He was the third generation in his family to run this ranch. Its care became his life's work.

I was an urban woman who handled horses at arm's length, who was only occasionally aware of sunrise, who thought of a 48-mile drive as an outing, and who certainly never imagined living in a place where picking up the daily mail would involve an hour's drive to the post office.

In Washington, D.C., in the spring of 1981, I did not know how dramatically my life would change. That I would adopt and be adopted by a new family, landscape, and life. And that in this new environment, the seasons would unfold one into another, seasons of raging wildfires, punishing early August frosts, blinding snowstorms, and choking dust.

I did not know that we as a family would face the pain of the farm crisis of the 1980s, scan the skies for dark rain clouds daily during seven years of drought, watch lamb prices then cattle prices plummet, and become a part of the debate over the use of western lands that would turn neighbor against neighbor.

Nor could I have imagined that I would walk through sage-scented hillsides surrounded by sky so blue and wide it stretched forever into silence and into my soul.

I could not have guessed all this in 1981. And I certainly did not know it was possible to become as connected to a place as I am now. But then in Washington, I am not sure I really understood the meaning of love, of home, of commitment. That would come to me here, 24 dirt-road miles from town.

Spring

IN THIS SEASON *the world turns from brown to green. The land is wet from snowmelt. Rushing waters spill over riverbanks. Sunshine stretches each day with light. We come back to the land slowly, tentatively, quietly. The earth is turned and seed is scattered into long rows. The animals arrive home from winter pastures. The world is young and new, full of secrets, full of second chances and birdsong.*

Beginnings

WITH THE MARKING of each new year with my husband at our sheep and cattle ranch in Idaho, I remember our beginning. Not the day we first met at the suggestion of a friend. That was December 30 and we were surrounded by Christmas lights and snow in the resort town of Sun Valley. Nor the subsequent days we spent together off and on that spring either in Idaho at his ranch or in Montana where I worked on a three-month assignment.

But rather I think about the days of that first spring, after the initial meetings. The time when I retreated from him to sort through dreams and choose the one that would inevitably change my life forever.

I had been wandering in heart and spirit. I had lived and worked for years in urban settings and was ready for change. Maybe I'd roam through olive trees in Greece for several months, find a small house and write. Or take a home by the stinging salt water of Seattle. Maybe I'd study dance in New York or food in France. I was ready for it all, between jobs. No ties.

Then my friend, kind and persistent over recent months, asked directly, "Well, have you ever spent a summer on a ranch?" Several months was all he proposed. He knew better than to bite too deeply into my days.

"You always lead the most romantic life," a friend in Washington, D.C., said when I told her I might spend the summer on an Idaho sheep and cattle ranch. I suddenly saw the offer in a new light. I called Idaho. "All right, I'm coming," I told him, as if it were a concession. "But just for the summer," I added quickly.

"I'll drive with my parents," I said. "They spend the summers in Oregon and every spring and fall follow the same route cross-country." I was predicting my time of my arrival.

The first day on the road was full of green. It was early summer in the East. On New York and New Jersey parkways, I marveled at the dense growth, especially chestnut trees heavy with cone-shaped pink and white blossoms. New Jersey bloomed with young crops of summer vegetables. "I have been unfair to New Jersey. It's not all oil refineries," I wrote in a journal from my lazy place in the backseat of the car.

That night I called Idaho. "We're at the Holiday Inn in South Bend," I told my friend. "Tomorrow Grand Island, Nebraska. It's always the same."

The next day was one of Illinois and Iowa greenness. Full sunshine over stalks of corn. The farms were larger, following straight section lines rolling across wide countryside.

In Grand Island, we sipped on drinks as we waited for our Holiday Inn dinner. I thought about the two remaining nights at similar motels with similar dinners before we'd reach Idaho. Then suddenly I grasped the expression on my father's face. It was shock. Both my parents stared at the end of the table. I followed their gaze to the form of my Idaho friend standing and smiling down at me, his cowboy hat still on his head. He had flown his small Cessna from Idaho to Nebraska to take me home.

My parents welcomed him enthusiastically as if he were an old friend from their past. In fact, only my father had known him from occasional western conference panel sessions on which the two men had served. Suddenly my mother excused herself from the table. "I've got to go call your sister," she announced. "This is the most romantic thing that has ever happened in our family. She won't believe it." I was speechless.

My friend dismissed his romantic, if impulsive, arrival, claiming he needed to look at cattle in South Dakota. I did not know then that this would be the first of many ranch business trips on which I would tag along in hopes of a quiet moment we could steal for ourselves. Nor did I know these experiences would allow me to become intimate with the landscapes of the West in a way few others can claim.

The next morning I wistfully waved goodbye to my parents as my friend and I climbed into his plane and lifted off the Nebraska runway for South Dakota. My parents headed for the interstate and their next stop, Cheyenne, Wyoming.

After a short flight, we were met by a farmer and cattleman from the small town of Hoven who had interested my friend in grazing livestock (in this case Holstein dairy heifers) on Idaho pastures. A year later this farmer would buy his cattle back and move them out.

We wandered through feedlots selecting the best heifers from the group. My friend told me what to look for: "the ones with a solid frame, good bones, a straight back." I trained my eye to these instructions and soon we had separated out 225 black-and-white beauties.

Late that afternoon in a local coffee shop, I listened to the farmer talk about growing up in this rolling plains country, as one of ten kids farming with his parents of German descent. I watched as he and my friend agreed to terms for the cattle and shook hands. My city ways suddenly crowded in.

"That's all?" I asked. The two men looked at me, startled. "You're not going to write this down?" I asked, unaware and certainly disapproving of the idea that rural business deals, no matter how sizable, could be finalized by a handshake and not a contract.

My friend and his new partner laughed as I began to write out the simplest outline on my yellow legal pad. We buy. One year later, the farmer buys back. Brief and spare but a contract. The men indulged me. It sounded reasonable on paper, but none of us could have predicted at the time how this deal would sour, that the earnest young man would be crushed by the farm depression of the 1980s, and that no amount of written agreements on yellow legal pads could save us in Idaho from the residual agonies of his losses in South Dakota. But that day under brilliant blue sky, life was full of possibilities.

The next morning, we flew off to Idaho. The cattle would be shipped by truck several days later. From the plane I stared, nose against the window collecting images of corn and wheat fields, of the rugged Black Hills, of Mount Rushmore with its massive, dignified heads carved into the granite mountain. It was a breathtaking flight.

We stopped for fuel in Gillette, Wyoming—"a disposable city" my friend noted as we stared at rows of trailers, housing for miners, that could be packed up and moved to a new town as soon as this coal deposit gave out.

Finally we reached Idaho and then the ranch. Circling wide, my friend pointed out fields of young alfalfa barely green, draws and ridges where cattle would graze later in the summer. We saw antelope along a hillside and circled Campbell Reservoir and creeks rushing full of water. It was late spring and everything was green and vibrant.

When he landed the plane and turned off the engine, I climbed out into a field of yellow sunflowers and amazing silence. We stood in the sunshine and let the stillness close around us. "We are home," he said.

In the distance I heard a new sound, a sandhill crane he told me, "from her nest on the meadow." As I listened I played with the idea that one day I might call this landscape home.

Coming to Flat Top

NOW THIS IS MY LANDSCAPE, this vast, open space. It's what people most remember when they visit our ranch—the expansive sweep of land rising and falling in every direction uninterrupted for miles. And overhead, a sky whose light marbles the earth through pale clouds.

From our cabin I can see mountains far to the east and north of us and basalt ridges and sagebrush hills to the south. But these merely bracket the open space.

Creeks with willows and cottonwood trees wind through the meadows and I often see antelope and deer with the livestock in the hills. But mostly I see sagebrush, tall grasses, and enormous space—everywhere. The Shoshoni and Bannock Indians knew this country intimately. So does my husband, and maybe someday I will too.

"I love trees," I told him on my first trip to his remote ranch. We were only 4 miles from town passing through the river bottom of a neighbor's land. It was thick with pine and aspen. We had 20 dirt-road miles to travel before we reached the ranch headquarters.

"You do, hmm—trees?" he questioned. "We don't have many trees at our place."

I had blundered. He was so anxious to show me the ranch and I had chosen the one landscape feature he could not provide. I retreated into silence.

The road began to climb, and as we reached the summit that divided the two properties I gasped. From there, for the first time, I could see immense space that extended east across rolling hills and ridges into the rugged Pioneer Mountains. Behind us the canyon ranch I had admired appeared small and pinched between forested hillsides.

As I scanned the beauty in front of me, my friend told the story of his grandfather, who at one time, with a neighbor, owned the land on both sides of the summit. When the partnership broke up, they divided the property. His grandfather chose the open spaces to the east because it was better livestock country.

As luck would have it, the narrow canyon land he gave up is now close to the resort community of Sun Valley and could sell for several times the amount of our ranch. But I wouldn't trade it for one acre of this vast landscape.

I admit there are days, when I return to the New England home where I was raised, that I thrill to the sight of thick greenness—sycamore, weeping willow, beech trees, flowering dogwood in spring, and bold red maples in autumn. In the East, trees are the landscape, forming it, framing it. But my delight is short-lived when on a sticky, hot summer day these same trees close in on me, competing for air, blocking the horizon, devouring the space.

Then I long for Idaho, where there is only an unobtrusive stand of cottonwoods along the creek behind our cabin to provide shade on hot summer afternoons. And I am free to stand on my front porch to reach my arms into vast space and touch forever.

The Cabin

OUR RANCH CABIN SEEMS ROOTED IN PLACE, as if it grew up from the earth. But in fact it was moved here over a hundred years ago by the original ranch owners, who carefully numbered and hauled each log from houses at the nearby abandoned Muldoon lead and silver mines and reassembled them here. Now it sits sheltered by towering cottonwood trees along a creek that runs behind it, and in front of it is the vast open space of tall grasses and rolling sagebrush hills.

It is really three cabins joined together in an L, with a porch tucked into its two outstretched arms. One side of this veranda is shaded by hop vines. The other is lined with hanging pots of flowers and is sunny much of the day. This is where I sit and listen to the stillness.

You enter the house through a screened porch where work boots stand along the inside log wall and hats hang above them. A back door leads to the creek and the hammock that sways between cottonwoods in the afternoon wind. A second door on the screened porch leads into the kitchen, the social center of the house.

This room is dominated by the large black Majestic-brand woodstove. Strings of chili peppers hang on the wall next to Indian baskets, and a long row of cookbooks lines the windowsill. Here shelves are filled with foods to appease any hungry whim—like Sunday morning *huevos rancheros*—out here, an hour's drive from the nearest restaurant or grocery store. There is a big table under two small-paned windows that look out onto the porch, and a large flower garden beyond.

The house extends in a narrow march through a hall into the living room, which we seldom use, preferring the warmth and smells of the kitchen. There is a large old rolltop desk along one wall with a television on top that picks up only a fuzzy picture from one faraway station. It is rarely turned on. The windows look out on the creek behind the house.

The L turns to the left, and immediately off the hallway is the tiny Lincoln room named for the bronze bust of Abraham Lincoln used to prop open the window on hot days. It was a bedroom in the past and now is my husband's office.

You cross through the pale green guest room to reach my workspace, a room with a large bookcase, contents spilling onto the floor, a long desk, and scraps of memorabilia tacked every which way to the walls and bulletin board. The door to the outside porch is almost always open to let in filtered light through the hop vines.

Ducking through a narrow bathroom you come to the end of the L—our bedroom. Here the view from the window gives the room its character, extending the small space into the fields and wildflowers, basalt ridges, and rolling sagebrush hills beyond. There are days when the warm sun touches the edge of the bed and I never want to leave that spot.

This is my home. It is not handsomely decorated or cleverly renovated. It is simply a hideaway, a place of quiet and space that I miss when events or seasons force us to leave. It is a home unlike any other I've ever had because it is an extension of the land on which it sits and often seems as rooted to the spot as the giant cottonwoods that sway above it.

Spring Search

"SURE COULD STAND A RAIN," my husband said, scanning the skies as if a storm might be just waiting for his call. "Sure could," his twenty-seven-year-old son, Tom, echoed.

It was late March. The three of us and our head cowboy stood outside the pickup. We were surrounded by a vast expanse of Idaho desert with its yellow and brown winter grasses and gray brush. Only a random butte formation and the faraway mountains to the north and south provided direction in this landscape that extended flat for miles. We were checking the range for our cattle before we brought them back from California winter pastures.

On this early spring afternoon, the wind was only a slight sound in the brush vying with faint meadowlark song for the stillness. A pale sun moved in and out of heavy clouds. The ground was the faintest green. The tiniest wildflowers pushed through the earth.

Years of drought had taken a toll on the land. The light snows and recent rains had not been enough to fill the lakes. They were empty—only shallow impressions in the dry earth. I watched my husband stoop and, with a stick, dig below the sandy soil. He hit hard ground within inches of the surface. "We really need a rain," he muttered.

The three men walked over to a water trough and leaned against the log railing that circled the tank. They discussed a water line, a fence, the best field for the first load of cattle. The wind tied itself around their voices and trailed the sound across the stillness. No one moved or talked too fast. "Good dry feed," I heard my husband say.

When I first came here I scanned the Idaho desert and saw only winter bleakness in the brown and gray March landscape. Not until I bent to the ground and watched my husband run his hand over the small green shoots did I see the new growth.

Each year we repeated this ritual and now my eyes, trained to wildness, saw the green even before I stooped to touch it. But I knew after several years of drought, this whisper of grass was no longer enough to bring us hope for the summer. Now we searched the skies for black clouds as well.

Sage Hens

"SAGE HENS," my husband said, jamming on the brakes of the pickup. We stopped abruptly along the side of the desert road and, as we did, the skies around the truck filled with fat brown birds startled by our presence. They swooped up then down again, landing just beyond our field of vision. My husband inched the truck forward and turned it off.

As the quiet caught up with us, we squinted into the brush where the birds had landed, but I saw nothing except late winter grasses, sagebrush, and patches of snow.

"The binoculars," he whispered as if the grouse might hear him in the enclosed cab of the pickup. He pointed to the glove box in front of me. "They're booming," he added almost breathlessly. It was their mating ritual. I knew it from pictures.

These outdoor experiences used to leave me in a quandary. I wanted to be excited when my ranch family recounted stories of wildlife sightings but years of city life had dulled my enthusiasm. There, my experience with birds had consisted of pigeons always underfoot in parks and public squares, and squirrels were the only animals I had seen outside of the zoo.

But after I moved to Idaho, my husband opened the wilds for me by pointing out deer on the meadows, elk in the hills, beaver dams and lodges on the rivers. Now, each summer, I strained to hear the early-morning call of sandhill cranes on our ranch meadows and watched the hillsides for antelope running free at sunset.

This flurry of birds excited me. I scanned the desert with the glasses until I saw one. A sage grouse, his white feathered lung pouches swollen with air. Then I saw another and another. They filled themselves then expelled the air, leaving a barely audible *whooop*. Their tails fanned up behind them, their wings flapped as they strutted smugly. Intrigued female birds appeared along a hillside.

A late-afternoon chill filled the truck as we leaned outside our windows straining to hear the faint booming sound. We sat there a long time, so far from ourselves, silent partners in the mating ritual. In the end, only darkness forced us back to paved highways and farm lights.

Farming

RECENTLY MY HUSBAND AND I stopped by a field to watch our son, Tom, getting the earth ready to plant grain. He moved up and down the long field on a large green and yellow John Deere tractor.

At the end of the row, he threw the levers and the huge tumble plow attachment on the rear with its four metal shears rose out of the ground while he turned the machine around. Tom shifted the lever again, and the plow shears flipped over and locked into place with a thud. The blades, now facing left instead of right, plunged back into the brown earth. I watched fascinated as it began again to churn up weedy grasses in front of it.

The large farming operation at our ranch was something of an enigma to me in the beginning. Not the procedures, but the enthusiasm my husband and our son had for this hard, sweaty, frustrating work. *That* was a mystery to me.

We raise hay and grain to feed the livestock that stay in Idaho over the snowy winters, enough to get them through until spring grasses come. We raise extra crops to sell: alfalfa if it's good quality will go to southern Idaho dairies; barley can be contracted locally to Coors or Anheuser-Busch; and there are always markets for wheat and rapeseed, now called canola. It seems these possibilities inspire the enormous energy and commitment to farming by the men in my family.

I guess I can understand the excitement when sprouts appear in long rows carved through rich brown fields. It is something akin to my reaction when zucchini seeds first push through the ground in my garden and weeks later when large yellow blossoms form green extensions.

However, farming is gardening on a scale I find overwhelming. For example, the watering, which in the dry Idaho landscape is a major undertaking. Dams in the creeks divert water into ditches that meander across meadows. When this is not possible, we use long hand lines connected to a pipe, connected to a pump—lines that are moved across large fields 50 feet at a time every 12 hours. Recently, after much family discussion, we invested in several expensive large pivots that spray water from suspended pipes that wheel automatically in a circle around large fields.

But I suspect son and husband are most intrigued by the machinery that makes agriculture happen: tractors, swathers, balers, and stackers. These huge mechanical beasts perform magic feats when they are not disabled in some isolated field, which seems to happen regularly, sending one or another of the men to some far-flung Idaho town for spare parts.

I'd be hard-pressed to say which machine the men think is the most fun. First the swathers cut through fields of tall alfalfa stalks, leaving a wake of long neat windrows. After the hay has dried for several days, the baler comes through, swallowing the loose hay, compressing it, then spitting it out in tightly wrapped bundles. Finally, stackers move across the fields, picking up the small bales and pushing them through the machine to a rear rack. When it's full, the rack will tip up to slide the hay onto a stack in a field or under a hay shed. The new, larger bales must be stacked individually with a front-end loader. Then there is the combine, which is used on loose crops like wheat or grass to extract the seed.

"Try it," my husband urges. So I bounce along on the edge of the driver's seat of the swather while he shifts and pulls levers. He tries to turn the job over to me. "Isn't it great?" he boasts of a long row of cut hay. I agree but refuse to be left alone in the machine. Just my luck to ram, jam, jolt, bolt, or overturn this expensive equipment and leave it in pieces.

In the end there is no denying the pride. After-dinner entertainment is a trip to check on the crops. In the dim light of early evening, my husband and I, with mother-in-law, son, and friends bounce in the pickup along rutted roads that follow fence lines or an irrigation ditch until we reach the right field. There we wander through the rows, picking a shaft of wheat or running a hand across small green alfalfa leaves. Often, in the center of the field we see a sleek sandhill crane, maybe two, settling into the silence.

In farming there can be a hailstorm or an early freeze that will wipe out a year of work in several hours, and there is the inevitability that crop prices will slump even lower this year. There are the long sweaty hours in the fields during planting season and round-the-clock work day after day during harvest.

The men in my family love it and every spring bring to it an unwavering optimism for a better harvest and higher prices. But perhaps I do understand farming—that it is, after all, the miracle of new growth and its promise that bring hope to them, like the early light of day when everything seems possible.

Camas

I SAW THEM IN MY MIND: my mother-in-law, Mary, and her friend Gertrude, both well into their eighties, two silver-haired women on shaky legs. They were standing in a sea of blue camas flowers on our ranch meadows. First I saw Mary at the wheel of her gray car driving it a bit recklessly off the dirt road to the edge of the blue field. I watched as she and Gertrude pulled themselves out of the vehicle, bent over the blooms, and snipped them off the stalk.

"Oh, they are so lovely," I heard one of them say, "so delicate."

"I've seen so few this year," the other added with a sigh, and her cane slipped from her hand, freeing it to gather the flowers more easily. Periodically one stopped, held a hand up to shield her eyes from the bright sun, and scanned the view. Their eyes take them where their legs no longer can.

I understood their joy. The camas always seem magic to me when I drive across the southern Idaho prairie named after this blue flower. In the late spring between Mountain Home and Fairfield on Highway 20, the landscape turns a lazy blue. As the car winds down from Cat Creek summit, I am caught off-guard by the spread of color. Is that a reservoir? New snowmelt? What body of water covers this pastureland? Then I remember. It is the camas and I am stunned by the sight of so many flowers at once.

The highway sign outside of Fairfield tells the painful story of the Bannock Indian Wars triggered by the camas root. Its bulb was an important food source for Native American people, who pounded it into a flourlike substance. As white settlers moved in, barbed wire appeared across landscape that had been wide open. Unable to live with the changes, several Bannocks killed a farmer's pig they saw rooting up precious camas bulbs. The army was called out to punish the Indians and war followed. It was the Bannocks' last stand to save their way of life before reservation confinement.

For several years I was alarmed to find only a small patch of camas when I drove across the prairie. Years of drought had siphoned life from these delicate flowers. And so I delighted in the patch of blue on our ranch meadow and understood the joy of the two silver-haired women, Mary and Gertrude, as they gathered the fragile blooms in the afternoon stillness.

Shipping the Sheep Home

HARD WORKING MORNINGS always begin early, 4 A.M. early, and this one is no different. We are loading our sheep onto trucks in the Panoche Hills of California for the trip home to Idaho. But first we must drive two hours south from the Bay Area to join the shipping.

The trucks are lined up a quarter of a mile from the Kamm exit off Interstate 5. We are in the heart of central California's farming and ranching country. The landscape is remarkably isolated for such a populous state, and from the exit, despite the distance, we can see the trucks across the flat farm fields. It is springtime green after days of heavy rain.

We drive to the temporary corral, slatted boards wired together that held the sheep overnight. The herders, our sheep manager, and the drivers are loading the first of five livestock trucks. The waiting vehicles stand along the dirt road, the stenciled lettering on their doors reading like a geography lesson: Scarpete and Sons, Cotati, California; Valley Livestock, Dixon; Peterson's Livestock, Carey, Idaho; Tri-Bell, Powell, Wyoming.

It is 6 A.M. when we join the team at work. My husband and our dog take up a position midway down the long alley. At the front are twenty sheep moving up the metal ramp to the top deck of the truck. When they are loaded, two herders open the first gate in the corral.

My husband calls out directions to the dog, who runs from side to side behind the next bunch of sheep to move them forward. Dogs are everywhere, running back and forth outside the gates, sailing up and over the corral fences, nipping here and there to herd the livestock.

The front sheep need coaxing to board the truck, unsure that this is the preferred option when green fields stretch out around them. A butt from behind pushes them forward. A trucker, crouched inside, counts as they enter the trailer, then cuts off the line when the compartment is loosely filled.

The men outside shoulder the ramp and move it down to the next deck, struggling under its weight, calling out to each other, "Little to the right, Shorty." "Up a little, Leon." We talk together as we wait for the truckers to replace the ramp.

"Just look at those lambs," Ben Elgorriaga says. He is the California sheep man who leases us pasture and, with our men, looks after our animals each winter. "One hundred forty pounds at least," he predicts. This is an impressive weight for a lamb, and it's Ben's way of boasting about the care he's given our animals.

When the last sheep disappears into the basket, the bottom deck of the last truck, two big Great Pyrenees guard dogs are loaded with them. Three sheepdogs are lifted to the empty compartment in the back of the truck, along with the herders' plastic brown suitcases bulging and strapped for the trip home to Idaho. The men ride in front with the drivers. Outside, bolts are fastened and locks clamped shut around the metal frame of the trucks. Then the vehicles pull away. But before they are out of sight, the remaining herders have dismantled the makeshift corral, returning the area to open space. It is only 9:15 A.M.

Now my husband and I are free to explore the isolated landscape of the Panoche Hills to the west of us. Much of the land belongs to Ben. It has been in his family for several generations and he knows its features acre by acre. He grew up here working sheep with his father, and now his sons work in the business with him. Ben's boyish, freckled face belies the fact that he has grown sons. He is a gentle man, confident and competent.

We listen to him when he says, "It is time for you to head north. The feed's getting old. The filaria grass is going to seed, and if the pods get tangled in the sheeps' wool, the value of the pelt will drop."

It is a brilliant blue day as we drive toward Ben's Panoche Hills. We take a road that winds around farms and grain bins. It is the only route open after heavy spring rains washed out other approaches.

We enter the canyon, then begin our climb up the road etched into deep green banks. The ascent turns steep and the terrain more closely resembles mountains than hills. Wildflowers are everywhere, splashes of color against the slopes, as if someone had thrown a can of yellow paint here, orange there, purple around the bend. As we near the summit the view turns gentle again, and the landscape becomes waves of soft, undulating hills merging one into another.

We drop into the next valley and stop at a sheep camp set against the flat bench of a hillside. There are three small cabins, a bathhouse, a bunkhouse with three bunk beds to sleep six, and the cook shack.

This last cabin is the largest. Its one room, painted white, holds a small gas stove, refrigerator and a long table covered with oilcloth. There are bottles of cooking oil and condiments stored on a corner shelf, and a blackboard on the wall with neatly written words, "Put away anything you use," in English, Spanish, and Basque. The windows around the cabin fill the space with light.

We walk to the edge of the bench where the land tumbles off to a distant valley floor. Far below, a herder with several dogs moves a band of sheep and the bell from the lead ewe bounces off the hills faintly. We sit in the sun without speaking.

Ben's Panoche Hills are a piece of history belonging to the sheep families of this sprawling state. And now this quiet, untouched place has ahold of us, as it does him. It is a landscape far different from our Idaho ranch, but it is just as much a refuge, a shelter, a safe place in a world spinning out of control.

Buying Bucks

ALMOST EVERY SPRING, soon after our sheep are home from California, we drive to Vale, Oregon, to buy Suffolk bucks, the black-faced male sheep we breed to our ewes. Swede Erstrom has some of the best in the region and we can quickly pick out twenty or so from him.

He got into the business when his son Pat's 4-H project grew into a flock of four hundred. Today the family has a reputable sheep outfit that father and son run together along with their farming operation.

At our ranch, we breed both black- and white-faced bucks to our ewes. We get the white-faced Rambolais or Columbia from Montana. Breeding these bucks will give us good lambs to replace older ewes. The sheep will be good mothers, herd easily, and provide a high-quality wool. The Suffolk black-faced bucks produce offspring with the best meat. The combination has earned us a reputation for fine Idaho lambs.

As we pull into the farm, deep blue skies and full sunshine belie the whipping wind that only hours earlier brought down thick tree limbs and billboards in the nearby town of Ontario.

I look for Swede's remarkable Border collie, Jiggs. Several years ago it was Jiggs who ran through the tall grasses gathering the bucks for us, needing only Swede's soft command "Bring 'em in, Jiggs" or "A little closer, now." We watched the dog take several steps using only that movement to push the sheep forward. Never rushed or rough.

This year the bucks are in the corral when we arrive and Jiggs is waiting patiently by Swede's side. Pat is with them.

The sheep are large, sturdy, clean, shorn, and ready for viewing. They are skiddish as they run or jump past us in a rush to get from one end of the pen to the other, where they huddle together anxiously. Swede is proud of his bucks and does most of the talking. His son Pat joins in only occasionally.

"Look here," Swede points to a prized animal. "See how wide he is across the loin. Look at his head, his long legs. His lambs will be big."

Swede's wife Mary joins us at the corral with Pat's four-year-old son, Kyle. They are three generations: father, mother, son, and grandson. Swede and Mary's modest cinder-block house is just beyond the pens. The yard is full of flowers and a yellow wild rose bush spills over the fence, a buffer between house and corrals, a sigh between living and working space.

"It was my uncle's," Mary tells me of the house. "My family lived down the road when we moved here in the late thirties. We came from eastern Colorado—dust bowl country," she adds.

In those days there was nothing but miles of desert. In the cool night air, families burned brush to clear the ground for planting. Then the irrigation ditches and canals were dug to bring water to the area, and electricity followed several years later. That's when the settlers felt the promise of their new home. And today we look across the sheep pens to the desert in bloom and green in the late spring with fields of wheat, onions, and beets.

After my husband chooses the bucks, Swede and Pat send the large animals down the chute to check them one more time before they brand them with black paint, marking them ours. Swede and Mary will drive them over to our ranch in several days. It is a kind of holiday for the couple.

The wind still whips the air as we climb into the pickup. And as we pull away from the farm I turn back to see three generations in the driveway, waving into the blue of the day with Jiggs standing next to Swede looking after us.

Wildflowers

I STARED OUT OF THE PICKUP WINDOW as we drove into our ranch, studying the landscape foot by foot beginning at the ridge line, down the slopes, across the wide pasture, until my eyes stopped at the side of the road. Then I retraced the path.

The land was a mass of color like nothing I'd ever seen before. Wildflowers hugged the earth, pink and white close to the ground at the edge of the road, then spiked purple-blue lupine led across the wide pastures into the foothills. There the ground suddenly turned brilliant yellow, splashed with sunflowers and balsamroot. After years of drought the color was a magnificent statement about life and survival.

"I have never, never seen the wildflowers like this year," my husband said. And even as we drove down the interstate outside of Boise he continued, "Look, look at the flowers out in the pastures. Wait till you see them at the ranch."

The magic started 150 miles later on the backroad to our home at about the spot where the pavement ends and the dirt begins. Here suddenly the scene became intensely brilliant with color. Even the spring grasses seemed greener than usual set off by fields of flowers.

We stopped for the bitterbrush—my favorite. Most of the year this plant blends unobtrusively with sage and rabbitbrush along the hillsides. But for a few weeks each spring it stands apart, its branches strung with fragile yellow blossoms that fill the air with a pungent sweetness. I look forward to days when my husband brings armfuls of these branches home to fill our cabin, even though we know the blossoms last only a moment. This day we gathered several sprigs to perfume the truck.

It was early evening when we crossed Friedman Creek. Only a trickle in last year's drought, now it spilled over rocks and rushed freely between its banks. The sky was full of clouds, pale pink in the late hour. We passed Cold Springs Corral, and my husband, unable to suppress his enthusiasm, said, "Wait till you see the next draw."

I peered out the window as we turned the corner to see a sweep of wildflowers from horizon to horizon, like the finale of a fireworks display. In every shape and color they tumbled down ridges we had hiked in summer months when the landscape was dusty and gray-green from its cover of brush. We stepped out into the evening air, smelled, touched a few blossoms near us.

It was then, with only meadowlark song breaking the silence, I remembered a recent radio report about grazing on public lands. An earnest environmentalist in San Francisco had said, "If only cattle ranchers could thrill to a hillside of wildflowers for the sake of the flowers, but they only see it as pasture for their cattle."

At the time, I was angered by her careless remarks, but on this day, standing in the tall lupine, I was simply bewildered. We were not the only ranchers who cherished the beauty of this spring. We all know well that as the wildflowers survived the drought, we too will survive and persevere, caring for this land because this is our home.

Boxes

RECENTLY, FRIENDS RIDING IN MY CAR had to squeeze in between two large lamp shades. They were less concerned about the tight fit than that they had ridden with the shades weeks earlier.

I admitted I was exhausted by the bulky objects myself. "They're in my car," I sighed, "because I'm going to the ranch and I don't want to leave them in town in the flurry of packing."

Most of my possessions, or those I think are imperative for survival, often nest in my car for weeks, if not months. It is because my husband and I move constantly—well, seasonally—in and out of our remote ranch. And it always seems that what I most want has been left behind. With everything in the car, I know where the important items are when I need them.

If we had our way, our family would stay at the ranch year-round, but each fall we are threatened by frozen pipes and icy weather at our uninsulated ranch house—elevation 6,000 feet.

And so, after we ship the livestock to winter pastures, we pack up the pickup and move to town. This means days of sorting through desk files, magazines, mail, books, clothes, canned food, and refrigerator leftovers. Anything that stays at the ranch must be unnecessary for five months and able to survive 20-below temperatures.

In spring, we repeat the process in reverse, and my pack rat instincts take over. What if I got to the ranch, way out there, and needed dishwasher soap or toilet paper or . . . green peppercorns? So I sort through winter supplies, stock up at the grocery store, pack up the contents of my desk and an extra roll of scotch tape just in case, and shoehorn everything into my car.

My husband is horrified. "You can get to town in an hour," he reminds me. "You don't have to take everything for the rest of your life." I agree with him as I throw an extra can of tomato paste into the last box, just in case.

Before I came to Idaho, I moved around a lot: California, Alaska, Montana, Washington, D.C. In lonely moments, I wondered if I'd ever feel at home anywhere. When I married my husband, a man intricately connected to the land, I breathed a sigh of relief. What could be more settled than a third-generation rancher?

That was before I emptied my first refrigerator and hauled my first box in and out of the car on an endless succession of seasonal moves. Then there are the several dozen road trips each year to check on the livestock that are wintering in warm climates more sensibly than we who stay behind in the Idaho cold.

I've learned a lot about stability since I moved into ranch life and I know it all comes down to this: if something is really important to me, like a toothbrush or a garlic press, I just pack it in a box and keep it in the car with me—all year.

Grandmother Peavey

WHEN GRAMS, MY HUSBAND'S GRANDMOTHER, arrived in southern Idaho in 1906, it was little more than an empty, flat expanse of sagebrush desert for miles in any direction. What despair must have filled her soul as she searched for beauty in the arid landscape so far from the green of north Idaho that she and her husband had left behind.

She had taught school in the small mining town of Wallace, where she was satisfied with friends and mountain stillness. But her new husband was an adventurer who heard that land was free for homesteading in the southern desert. And so they moved.

They staked out a place and gave it their surname, Peavey. The homestead was near the present-day site of Twin Falls and near the spot where the Snake River winds through deep canyons and cascades over steep rock falls. Later, their homestead and the surrounding area developed into the small town of Peavey for a whisper of time and Grams became its postmaster.

Grams gave birth to her first child after traveling by train 120 miles across the desert to the town of Pocatello and the nearest hospital. She later carried the child with her in a basket as she planted Lombardy poplars to define the borders of their homestead.

In the beginning, she and her husband knew so little about what they were doing that they bought a steer, thinking it was a bred milk cow, and spent a lot of time waiting for the animal to calve and give milk. In later years this was her favorite story and she'd laugh again with each retelling.

Grandmother Peavey died nineteen days after she turned one hundred. She had three days of birthday gatherings with family and friends from around the country, and now they say she died from too much partying. I met her only once, at one of the birthday celebrations. But I think of her each time I pass the park in the city of Twin Falls.

The story goes that after she arrived in this desert landscape, her despair was so great, her husband took her to see the new park in town. It was no more than a staked-off area of sagebrush and ankle-deep dust. "If that's ever a park," she challenged him, "I'll eat the grass." "It will be," he promised her. "If not, we will leave."

Indeed, in time the roped-off land turned green, and today the park flourishes with its tall shade trees, flowers, sweeping lawn, and a band shell for summertime concerts. It provides relief in a city whose boulevards strain with commercial expansion, where the latest fast-food restaurants and motel chains crowd the edges of newly ploughed rich, brown fields.

In the early years the park brought solace and a promise of greenness to Grandmother Peavey. Today it does the same for those who follow her, serving as a sanctuary from the gathering urban sprawl of this southern Idaho town.

Those We Lost

ONCE, I TOOK OUT A LOAN. I was in my early twenties and it seemed the thing to do to escape an immediate financial crisis. But I'll never forget my fear of the balding man behind the desk. I felt humbled and humiliated by his questions and I rushed to repay the $300 to retrieve my life from his hands.

With this rather inconsequential history behind me, I was stunned to step into the world of agriculture in the early 1980s. I quickly learned how dependent neighbors and friends were on financial loans to sustain their farm operations. Their choice of crops, numbers of livestock, their very livelihood, depended on the judgment and goodwill of their bankers.

And that was about all they could depend on in the 1980s. With a national farm policy gone awry, prices plunged to record lows. Soon, with little money coming in on crops, farmers found themselves unable to repay bank loans. A strange, new dance ensued between farmer and banker—a dance of survival. Bankers threatened foreclosure. Farmers responded with bankruptcy.

I was working for a farm organization at the time with ranchers and farmers, many of whom faced ruin. Nationally, they left the land in droves—more than 700,000 of them. In Idaho we struggled to save our people.

I often wonder if anyone will tell the story of those years, of the farms that were lost, of short-term decisions made by bankers worried about their bottom line, decisions that would seal the fate of many families. Of husbands, wives, children torn apart by fear. Of towns that emptied and shops that were boarded up. Of neighbors so terrified by what they saw that they turned against one another without compassion, issuing blame as if this could save them from a similar fate.

The drought finally broke the cycle, making those few crops that survived valuable again. But the losses left deep scars, and today less than 2 percent of Americans are still farming. Now, I wonder, did we learn anything?

I did. I learned from them all, especially the ones we lost. I learned about home. Our ranch is a new place to me because of them, and I now absorb with a quiet urgency the stillness of our land, the sweet smell of sage, the call of sandhill cranes on our meadows, and the pale light that settles over the vast space each evening.

Burley

WHEN I FIRST MOVED TO IDAHO, I spent a lot of time following my husband around his ranch operation, trying to understand this new life lived on the land. In the spring this meant time at the Kimama headquarters.

Often at the end of the day, it would be too late for the long drive north and we'd spend the night in Burley, 15 miles south of the farm. Over the years, I got to know this busy agricultural town although my view was, and still is, that of an outsider.

Burley, with its skyline of silos and grain elevators, was a service center for the farms that stretched along the Snake River. Its two main highways marched at angles past stores selling irrigation equipment, fertilizer, and farm machinery until the streets intersected at the city center. Banks, specializing in farm loans, clustered at its midpoint with an occasional floral or sewing shop settled into a nearby storefront. Recreational shopping was limited in Burley.

But after the sun went down, things were lively. Most of the activity took place at the Fifth Amendment bar, a wild and wooly cowboy watering hole. It was always smoky and loud, throbbing with country and western music and reckless talk. Girls in miniskirts spun on barstools flirting with local farm boys in snug wranglers and fancy boots. My husband would point to a stool at the end of the bar and tell me, "Baxter Black used to sit there and tell stories all night long, when he worked as a vet for Simplot . . . before he got famous," he added. The Fifth Amendment seemed as essential to the community as the farm supplies along the main highways of town.

Burley, like many agricultural communities, strained to survive the farm depression of the 1980s. Its chamber of commerce pursued economic alternatives, such as turning the annual Snake River boat races into a national event and enticing tourists off the highway to visit its City of Rocks. A Wal-Mart opened. The resuscitation seemed to be working.

This spring I returned to the town for the first time in several years. While my husband was at the farm, I wandered the streets, noting several small *taqueria* stands scattered around town and the Mexican social hall at its center. The streets were lightly traveled, and many downtown buildings looked abandoned.

I stopped in a small Mexican café and watched the high school–age daughter helping her mother. In her free moments this pretty girl sat in a nearby booth and stared out the window. For whom or what was she waiting? Were her dreams on these quiet afternoon streets?

That night my husband and I ventured into a new restaurant. The room was empty except for its owner seated at the bar staring out the window. He was Vietnamese.

Suddenly I realized that this was the Fifth Amendment cowboy bar. Its new owner was sitting where Baxter Black had spent so many nights telling stories. A long buffet table filled with exotic dishes covered the parquet dance floor. Harsh bright lights begged intimacy. The owner shuffled across the room to turn on a wide-screen TV as if its familiar images would make the Guoi Cuon and Bang Xao seem less foreign to us.

Where had everyone gone? I wondered. Was there another Fifth Amendment now, or was this the result of the 1980s farm depression? Had change eaten away at rural America so slowly that we have yet to see which families, which communities, have been lost and which ones found?

And it was as if I could see the two cultures dancing silently across the floor. One familiar, one foreign. One trying to understand, the other waiting to be understood.

Sheep Tragedy

AND SO INTO THE UNPREDICTABLE, springtime desert our sheep return from California. Often they tumble out of livestock trucks after the twelve-hour ride into sunny, warm days, sometimes they face chilling winds. But this year the worst happened: they arrived home in the midst of a cruel spring snowstorm, April 9.

I heard the story over the phone, miles away visiting my parents in Connecticut. My husband, still shaken several days after our tragedy, told me of what he called "the storm that would do January proud."

"It seems everyone in the sheep business has something like this happen at least once in a lifetime," he said. "Fire, storm, predators. This is my once, I guess, and now never again."

Then he told me the story of our sheep trucks caught in the raging snows south of Twin Falls. It was the same storm that had traffic backed up on Interstate 84 from Twin Falls to Burley, a distance of 35 miles. It was the storm that had blown over a long-haul truck on the Perrine Bridge north of town that morning. The livestock drivers with our sheep, alarmed by fierce winds that blew snow across roads and hard into the windshield, decided to take the backroad to the interstate, to steer away from spinning, weaving vehicles out of control on the highway.

As they drove the quiet alternate route, a garbage truck came toward them straddling the center line of the two-lane road. In a split second the first livestock driver saw the vehicle, swerved onto the shoulder, then over-corrected. The trailer crashed to its side, sheep thrown one on top of another, decks collapsed. The animals panicked, fell, kicked, stood, and fell again until the struggle subsided. In the end, two hundred of our sheep were dead, suffocated in the capsized cargo space.

My husband waited for the truck at a designated intersection

30 miles north. He received the chilling phone call and rushed south to face the tragedy. Alone with the drivers of the two livestock trucks, he moved through dead sheep "often five animals deep" to pull a live ewe or lamb out from under heavy, lifeless bodies. He paused on the phone, barely able to go on.

"Half the animals died," he whispered. "Now there are ewes without lambs, lambs without mothers. We can only hope the young are old enough to survive on hay and spring grasses without milk." I imagined the snow flying fast and hard, hitting the truck in a staccato tempo, the wind whirling, shrieking as if to cover the sounds of bleating sheep that were confused and frightened by the death around them.

It is the kind of experience that happens in ranching, an industry where birth and death fill our everyday lives. But it is rarely this cruel and even now, weeks later, it is a story that is hard to tell. And it will be years before I forget the sound of my husband on the phone, his pain and disbelief. "Once in a lifetime," he said quietly, "is too much. I pray, never again."

Laidlaw Park Range Tour

MY HUSBAND AND I WERE AT A MEETING of farmers from the Laidlaw Park Grazing Association. We had gathered in the spotless living room of the Mecham farmhouse. Its large front window looked out over lawn and fields, and its rear window by the dining room table took in the vegetable garden plot not yet planted for this year.

The conversation moved slowly, leaving me time to glance around the room. It was full of sofas and armchairs; a piano filled one wall. Propped on the closed keyboard was a small unframed canvas, a scene like several others on the wall. They appeared to be replicas of Idaho postcards, mountains, pine trees and lakes painted in oils with exacting attention to detail. On the top of the upright piano, an ivy plant extended runners across the top and down the sides in a determined march to the floor.

The eight men gathered in the room, all in flannel shirts, jeans, and work boots, talked about the Laidlaw Park spring range tour. As is often the case in agriculture these days, none of the men was young, but rather middle-aged to graying. The BLM range manager from the Shoshone district office had driven up this Saturday to join the meeting.

While the men talked about water tanks, fencing, and feed; about running cows and calves versus steers; about the condition of the middle east field and the thumb of the park, Cloyd Mecham sat at his dining room table taking notes. His gray hair was neatly in place, his glasses steady on the end of his nose. Cloyd knows what he's doing. After all, he's been the association's secretary for fifty-three years and he's taken a lot of minutes.

This year at their spring meeting, the Laidlaw cattlemen had decided to invite environmentalists to join the annual land inspection. One rancher called it "a beginning to talk to each other, get away from some of the hostility, and see what's happening on the land." But others in the association were skeptical.

We were a member of the group made up of livestock producers who live around the small town of Carey. We grazed cattle from the high desert country to the foothills of the Pioneers. From April to June each year, as a cooperative group, we took our animals to the public lands of Laidlaw Park, a remote round of BLM desert and lava rock country. A cowboy watched over the cattle and hauled water to them.

Most of the cattlemen were small operators, third- and fourth-generation family farmers. They owned home ranches where they raised hay and grain to hold their animals through the winter. And they grazed the rest of their private land all summer.

But in the spring, when their own feed was not ready, they depended on the desert. This time allowed them to ranch the rest of the year. Now these men were fearful of the growing disapproval of their place on public lands and had decided to bring their critics along for the tour.

A week later we met again, the night before the Laidlaw Park range tour, for the briefing. This time there were eighteen of us. We gathered for pizza in a town north of Carey—husbands and wives, all association members, plus BLM personnel and environmentalists.

The range manager showed maps and explained that Laidlaw Park is one of the world's largest *kaipukas*. Kaipukas, he added, are rich grassy areas completely enclosed by lava rock as the result of volcanic activity. They have been found throughout the southern Idaho desert, and some of them, in their isolation, had become small laboratories of natural vegetation.

At dinner, the ranchers talked about the number of cattle they grazed each year. "I think you'll find the park's in real good shape," commented the Shoshone district range manager, explaining that the ranchers had decided to put out fewer cattle than the BLM allowed in order to protect the land during the recent drought years. There were questions about species of grasses and the effect of severe fires that recently tore across the landscape.

The next morning we met in Carey to board the government vans. It was a good chance to talk to one another. The gathering now included some sheep men who ran their animals in the park on their migration north each year. Several other members of the cattlemen's association also joined the tour, standing apart, shy and wary of the strangers.

Laidlaw Park is acessible by dirt road but once inside its circle, the 100,000-acre area becomes a labyrinth of rock outcroppings and buttes that mimic one another, rising and falling, blocking horizons, and confusing bearings unless you know the area intimately. I will not go far into the park alone.

We drove most of the day, stopping to look at the grasses and plants and first touches of wildflowers, checking the lakes for water. There were questions and answers and some debate, but mostly just talk.

Even now I don't know if the experience changed any minds, but at least the sides took on names and faces. At these events there is rarely press interest, no incendiary speeches or demonstrations, so there are no television cameras. Just people of the West standing side by side on the land.

Here in the quiet landscape, angry voices are muted and accusations merge with circumstance. It must start this way if we are to understand and save the land.

Sandhill Cranes

I WALK ACROSS THE LAWN outside our ranch cabin in the pale light of early morning. At first there is no sound and I tiptoe as if I might disturb the quiet. Then the silence is broken by the warbling call of sandhill cranes, the most splendid of birds around our ranch. I don't see them but I know they are not far off, probably in the field just beyond the dirt road to the lower ranch.

This year there are more sandhills than anyone can remember. Earlier in the week, we marveled at twelve pairs gathered in a newly plowed field at dusk. Sometimes, like now, we may not see them but we are hushed by their remarkable call filling the air. Then we squint across fields for a glimpse of them, their long thin necks stretching skyward, their rounded bodies balanced on spindly stick legs. When they take off, the birds fill the sky with their huge wings, swooping low and stately over the fields of tall grasses that hide their young.

Their calls bounce off the landscape, filling the air with possibilities of places they've been and have yet to go on their annual spring migration, which covers thousands of miles. Some will stay on our vast, open ranch meadows, others will travel farther north.

This morning I hear them and hold my breath. Their sound is a part of the silence, a part of the morning light, a part of the space. I could stand here for hours if schedules would not intrude, if the phone would not ring, if there were no meetings and people calling for help—save our water, save our schools, save our freedoms, save our silence.

I remember when I worked with farmers how reluctant they were to leave the land to protest policies destroying their industry. But I understand. I often feel that way too. When there are mornings of sandhill cranes and evenings of pale sunsets that insulate us from the debate, it seems irreverent to violate the quiet. Yet I have learned I cannot protect these treasures if I don't leave to tell their stories.

Now I listen—absorbing the sandhill call, unwilling to begin my day. For just a moment longer, I hold on to the stillness.

Laidlaw Fence

As SPRING IS DRAGGED KICKING AND SCREAMING into existence this year, we try to ignore its petulant behavior, its ice storms, snow flurries, its damp cold days. Instead we begin the chores of the season. The sheep are just back from California and the cows with their calves are just released from their winter pens in southern Idaho. They line up in fields along the edge of the desert looking northward to the snow-covered mountains where they'll spend the summer.

They seem impatient to get home, like dogs and mushers straining at the starting line before the Iditarod. They stir around, mothers nibbling the spring green grasses, with young at their sides.

But it is not time to move yet. The deserts are full of feed while snow still covers much of our summer range. There are animals to be doctored and of course fences to mend before the animals return home.

Checking and fixing fence is as much a part of spring as the snow runoff. But there is one meadow where the fence is ready, is always ready, for the animals when they arrive home each year. It is the Laidlaw fence that surrounds over 4,000 acres of land at the heart of our ranch.

It was built by the original ranch owner of our place, a Scotsman named Jim Laidlaw, who was determined to keep coyotes away from his prized sheep and best pastureland. Laidlaw was a pioneer in the sheep business who developed the Panama breed of white-faced ewes and introduced the black-faced Suffolk bucks into Idaho. He was not about to watch his valuable animals fall prey to marauding coyotes.

So he designed and built a fence up to the task. And today, some seventy-five years later, this fence still stands, strong and imposing, defining the wide boundaries of a meadow that contains some of the best grazing land and fields of crops on our place.

The most notable feature of the fence may be its massive Douglas-fir corner posts, each one 2 to 3 feet in diameter. When it was built, the ends were lightly burned to form a charcoal seal to protect them from rotting. Then these huge posts were sunk deep into the earth with Jim Laidlaw coaching, "Dig 'er a little deeper, boys."

What is less obvious about the structure are the fourteen strands of wire strung between the posts. There are four barbed wires, two planted underground to keep the coyotes from digging beneath the fence and two strung along the top. These fortify the ten spring steel wires running horizontally between. Wooden posts and metal stays at regular intervals hold these in place.

The 16-mile fence cost $1,000 a mile to build, an enormous amount at the time. And today, it needs little repair, only an occasional staple.

Neighbors still admire its workmanship and strength three-quarters of a century after it was built, and still comment on the scope of the project, sometimes poking fun. "I have to wonder," one of them said recently, "if in the end, old Jim Laidlaw didn't fence in almost as many coyotes as he fenced out."

Snakes

I WAS WALKING ALONG THE RANCH DIRT ROAD that ambles beside Friedman Creek through willows and cottonwood snags and past beaver ponds, when I was suddenly struck with the thought that snakes might be lurking around me. I'm not sure what provoked the idea, but the brush on either side of the path seemed at once alive with almost everything, especially rattlesnakes, and I realized that in this rolling, open country, I had no place to hide.

As a child, my fear of snakes was immediate when at age seven I peered into the glass enclosure at the San Diego zoo and recoiled at the sight of a twisted sequined reptile wrapped around a rock. I didn't sleep for nights afterward.

But my worst fears were realized several years ago on our annual spring cattle drive. It was our first day out on the desert, and as always my husband was circling the starting field in his plane to make sure the cowboys had found all the cattle scattered in the lava rock below.

This day, he spotted our black and white Border collie staggering in the brush. He dropped a note from the plane to his son on horseback. "Something's wrong with the dog." Then he flew to the desert airstrip to get his pickup. When his son found the dog, the beautiful animal was gasping for air and shaking under a sagebrush. He cradled the collie for a half hour until he saw my husband's truck pass on the road. Tucking the dog in the shade, he jumped on his horse to catch his dad. When they returned, the dog was dead.

When my husband told me softly from the doorway of the camp, I could not believe him. I was cooking lunch for the cowboys. "It was a rattlesnake," he whispered. I shuddered. This had been my first dog, a loving animal, still young, and in the morning stillness with only the sound of meadowlark song to cover my sobs, my husband and I held each other.

Riding

"LET GO OF THE HORN," my husband called out. "I can't," I wailed from the back of the galloping horse who, only moments before, had been described to me as a kid's horse. But that's the way it was with Sin, named because he was uglier than sin with his one red-rimmed blue eye and one brown. A short, stocky strawberry Roan, he'd amble so slowly he'd have to run from time to time to catch up. It was a matter of style.

In the early days when I had just moved to the ranch from city life, I was assigned a string of old wrecks to ride, all just like Sin. As we rode along on our annual, five-day, spring cattle drive, no amount of kicking, coaxing, or yelling could hasten the lazy creature beneath me. And as I fell farther and farther behind, my chances of graduating to a more capable horse diminished commensurately.

I watched the riders from a distance until suddenly, I was startled into a panic when "my" horse broke into a gallop stumbling over lava rock and low brush to catch up with the other riders. I grabbed the saddlehorn and held on for dear life. After all, what else could that protrusion be for? I reasoned.

"Let go!" my husband yelled across the field.

"I can't!" I yelled back in terror as my horse raced on.

But then there came the glorious day when friends from town joined us for the desert crossing. "Well, no, we haven't really been on a horse before," they admitted as they pulled on their boots at 5 A.M.

So it happened. They were put on the "gentle" horses and I got to move up to Charro. This horse was a wonder. Easily a hand taller than the other animals, he had a spirited walk and was eager to move the cows as quickly as possible.

I sat tall, held the reins easily, and guided him from side to side behind the livestock. We could be trusted to ride the fence to keep the animals out of a neighbor's field and to hold a hundred head back while the front cows crossed the highway. And when Charro took off on a gentle run, it was several moments before I realized that I hadn't even reached for the saddlehorn.

"How amazing!" I remember thinking as I eyed the braided rope coiled flat by my knee. Hmmmm. A lariat. Maybe even that . . . someday.

Cattle Drive

EVERY SPRING WE MOVE OUR CATTLE 50 miles across open desert, ranch hands on horseback with dogs at their heels. We pull a cow camp for a headquarters. The trip can take from three days with the steers to five days with the cows and calves. We are a strange sight, a pilgrimage of sorts, of animals and men moving north for the summer to high country, green pastures, and mild days.

The timing of the cattle drive depends entirely on feed and water for the livestock. This year my husband and I check the route several times. It is silent, wild lava rock and sagebrush country. The grasses are good but lakes normally full of water are empty. It will be another drought-year crossing.

The first day of the drive, we gather the cattle at our winter headquarters north of Burley along the edge of the Snake River plain. From there we begin the move north toward the snowcapped Pioneer Mountains in the distance.

Throughout the next few days, we follow rock outcroppings, lakes, and buttes across the desert. It is the route used by Idaho sheep outfits for years. We all must know the trail well because the desert is a deceptive place.

At first glance it appears to be a flat tangle of sagebrush filling in the expanse between mountains to the north and south. But look again. Here is a rise and fall where from a distance it appeared flat. A lava rock outcrop pushes up from the earth burned and split open like a loaf of country black bread. Its center is hollowed like a crater, its entrance is split rimrock forming a narrow canyon.

Across the desert the pattern is repeated. A mass of rock forms a rounded butte here, a long low outcropping there—Wildhorse, Sand, Steamboat, and Wagon Buttes—rises and depressions cut into and pushed out of this complex desert landscape.

And in this illusive country, I suddenly understand how men have lost their bearings and disappeared for days. How cattle who stray from the herd are trapped in rocks and left behind. How only those who have an intimacy with the land can find the old Indian springs with cold drinking water hidden in lava rock caves. How only those who travel this country for years know its landmarks.

Yet it is not a frightening landscape. Look down at the smallest details, slow to reveal themselves. Wildflowers, pink, yellow, blue, some no bigger than a fingertip hidden among stalks of purple larkspur and lupine. And the grass is green now, green for a whisper of time each spring, then brown too soon. Smell the sage as it fills the air with its haunting fragrance. Listen to the silence, watch the light spread across the landscape, its patterns stretching, shifting with the hours of the day. This is the Idaho desert.

The first day, we pass Steamboat Lake by midmorning, the cattle strung out in a long line. They say the area was named by a sheepherder who reported that a heavy snowmelt filled the lake enough to float a steamboat. The story seems bittersweet as we pass the dry lakebed this drought year.

At noon, we stop at McRae Lake for sandwiches. The cattle drink from metal troughs hauled in and filled by ranch hands earlier in the day. We might camp here on the butte above this wide lake in a normal year, but today we push on, leaving behind the empty bed, kicking up dust devils in the morning wind. We accelerate our move to the high country.

The cattle string out again along the narrow road, the only trail through the east–west stretch of jagged lava rock, lustfully named the "Tetons" by old-time sheepherders. There is little sound, only faint birdsong and occasional wind brushing through the sagebrush.

Several hours later we spot the cow camp on a rise in the distance. This wooden trailer, pulled each day by a pickup to our next overnight spot, is our headquarters. Inside there is a small cooking area in the front of the camp, a table and benches that pull down from the wall in the center, and bunk beds in the back of the wagon.

After supper dishes are cleared away, cowhands and friends along for the ride, sometimes as many as twelve of us altogether, gather again at the table to play or watch a little gin rummy, maybe a bet or two, with faces half-hidden in the shallow light of a lantern hung from a ceiling hook. And there are stories—lots of stories—of other crossings.

The next morning, when I start the bacon frying at 4 A.M., I hear the muffled voices of the men outside watering and saddling their horses in the dark. They come in to warm up, splash water from a tin basin on their hands and faces, then sit down under the lantern to eat. No one talks much.

By 5 A.M. we head out on horseback to round up the cattle that have wandered during the night within the several miles between the natural barriers formed by lava rock outcroppings. We are silent in the morning stillness, savoring the newness of the day, the smell of sagebrush bursting under our horses' feet.

Within an hour the air has warmed enough for us to shed our jackets and we tie them onto the back of our saddles. We may ride together for a while, two here, three there. "They're moving right out this morning," Max says. "It's going to be a hot one," he adds a little later. Then we split off again, mostly preferring the quiet of the desert. We ride far enough behind the animals not to crowd them. Later in the day the cattle will grow tired and need to be pushed, but not now. That night we camp at Wagon Butte and water the horses at the nearby Indian well.

The next day we pass Sand Flat and look north over the vast green meadows called Phildelphie Flats by the locals, now renamed Paddleford by the BLM. It is the first break in the desert and a sign the small farms of Carey are just ahead.

It is late afternoon when we cross Highway 20, the short route between Boise and Yellowstone Park. People pull their cars over to take pictures of cowboys and cattle crossing the asphalt. The world crowds in with the urgency of daily life.

We look back to the desert one last time—a place without barbed wire, without phones or people. A place of sweet-smelling sagebrush and silence broken only by birdsong. We are dusty and tired but changed by the experience, slowed by it, moved by it. It is a second home to us and every year we leave it, and springtime memories, reluctantly.

Gourmet Food

I REMEMBER MY FIRST SPRING CATTLE DRIVE after I moved to Idaho. At noon each day, I arrived at our camp with the other cowhands, hot and dusty, only to wonder who in their right mind could eat all that food on the table. It had been laid out by the wife of our head cowboy, who had spent all morning cooking and now stood by the stove watching us eat in silence. And I remember a half hour later wondering how I could get back on my horse slinging an extra 20 pounds of biscuits, pot roast, gravy, and pie with me.

Then came the year I was asked to cook and the tiny cow camp kitchen was turned over to me. But before I could seriously consider this new assignment, the phone rang. It was my mother-in-law. "Now don't you go cooking any of your gourmet meals," she warned. "Those cowboys won't eat that stuff and they've worked hard. They need a good meal."

I was offended. Did she think I would serve quiche and fruit cups for heaven's sake? I knew cowboys eat only plates of meat, potatoes, and biscuits. I took up the challenge.

Several days later she called again. "Don't you fix those boys your gourmet food," she continued, as if there had been no two-day interval. I politely reminded her that I had been on three cattle drives myself and knew my role.

Smugly, I started my shopping list and congratulated myself after successfully surviving the bulk foods grocery experience. I rather liked the startled looks people gave me as I loaded the pickup with staggering amounts of eggs, meats, potatoes, coffee, bacon, bread, cold drinks, ingredients for cakes and brownies, and finally a head of lettuce and a few zucchinis for a little fresh produce. The small cow camp kitchen was short on space for perishables.

Before I headed out to the camp there was one last reminder. "Don't you," my mother-in-law began, and I joined in, "serve those boys that gourmet food," we completed in unison. But I must confess it was only several days later, as I was swearing at the lumps in the pot roast gravy, that I had to wonder if pesto wasn't easier to make after all.

That year I had not been home twenty minutes from the cattle drive when the phone rang. "You fed those boys meat and potatoes, didn't you?" came the greeting through the phone. "Who is this?" I asked, just to be perverse.

And the ritual continued for another six years until, hearing no complaints from the cowboys, her warnings stopped.

Then one night around the dinner table, stories about the old days came tumbling out. My husband began, "Remember, Mom, when you came to the ranch to cook for the cowboys one spring?" I came to attention. "We ate turkey for three days and turkey soup for another week until we lost half the crew." My mother-in-law laughed and took up the story. "'Ma'am, we eat meat and potatoes,' one of them told me. 'We don't eat no soup.'"

I was stunned by this story. And I suddenly realized that my mother-in-law had not been riding me all that time because she thought I was an outsider. In her own way she was just passing on her best ranching experience, and it had taken me all these years to understand.

Floods

DAY AFTER DAY IT RAINS. Dirt turns to slick mud, then into dark brown pools. Water spills out of city gutters onto busy streets. But on the desert, lakebeds drink in the moisture after seven years of drought.

My husband scans the black skies. "These rains can be dangerous," he says. "It was like this in 1982 when floods took out the dams on Little Fish Creek and water poured through Carey."

I understood. High southern slopes, usually melted bare by now, are covered again by late-spring snows. This doubles the volume of melt when warm weather comes.

I remember 1982. My husband and I flew over our ranch headquarters at Muldoon to check the creeks and rivers for signs of spring. Instead, even from our height, we saw that the rock and dirt wall of Campbell Dam had broken and water was rushing through the gaping hole.

We flew back to town, where my husband dropped me off and gathered his boots and shovel into the pickup. Then he retraced our route, this time driving north from Carey. The mud made the road to the dam impassable so he hiked cross-country the 3 miles. Dragging the long-handled shovel in one hand, he climbed up and over the ridge line through sage and rabbitbrush, sucking mud, and wet snow, often sinking up to 2 feet.

At the dam he raced against the surging waters, struggling alone to fill the hole in the dirt wall, first with rocks, then with mud, knowing he had to be faster than the water pushing from the other side. When he was done, exhausted and wet, he hiked the rugged 3 miles back to his truck.

But instead of returning to town, curiosity drove him farther into the ranch to check Friedman Creek, which only hours earlier, as we saw from the plane, was still contained within its banks. Now he saw waters easily 300 yards wide and several feet deep spilling across the road and surrounding fields. Frightened by such speed and struck by a sense of foreboding, he turned south to Carey. He was unaware as darkness settled over him that he was only moments ahead of rushing water so fierce it had taken out two other dams, and was sweeping trees, willows, and boulders larger than cars down the valley behind him.

He would not know until the next day the extent of these angry waters and how narrowly he had escaped with his life.

"It will take years to heal the damage from these floods," my husband said. And I am reminded again that the land that fills our lives is not really ours. We care for it but we can never anticipate or control its reckless moods.

100 Degrees in the Shade

IT WAS HOT. There was no other way to describe the afternoons on our recent cattle drive 50 miles across the southern Idaho desert. Early in the morning it was clear and warm. That was the first bad sign.

In the 4 A.M. darkness, we drank coffee from enameled tin cups in short-sleeved shirts as the cowboys muttered, "Should be colder than this now." We were usually wrapped in jackets at that hour.

It had been cool enough early in the day, but by 9:30 the sun was strong and riders were reaching into saddlebags for their water bottles. The cowboys wore felt hats to water the working dogs, punching down the crown from the outside to form a bowl. By late morning we were all hot and thirsty and eager to reach the day's destination by noon.

"Keep those coolers out of the sun," I barked as we unloaded them from the camp wagon. And although we put them in the strip of shade thrown by the camp trailer, that shade moved rapidly and we pushed the ice chests around in hot pursuit.

On this trip, the water buckets always seemed low; empty pop cans piled up at an alarming rate. I made gallon after gallon of iced tea. We couldn't get enough liquids.

Finally some of us headed for a trailer at the edge of town that belonged to one of our crew. "There's no furniture, no lock on the door, and only cold water in the tub," the cowboy warned us, but the water sounded too good to pass up.

There was a bloodcurdling holler from the first man into the tub. "This isn't cold," he yelled. "This is ice." But that didn't stop any of us when our turn came to splash the rushing tap water over ourselves in an effort to lower our body temperature. It was, we learned, over 100 degrees in town and hotter on the desert.

By the time we got back to camp, the sun had weakened with the late hour and the desert colors were spreading across the vast, flat landscape.

It was one of the trips on which I was reminded of the importance of water and the complexity of life-and-death struggle to live in an arid landscape—a country where, Will Rogers said, "whiskey's for drinking, water's for fighting for."

That spring we suffered the effects of a winter without snow. On that cattle drive, we passed one dry lakebed after another over four days, hauling water to fill troughs for the animals to get them through the heat and dust.

We hauled water for ourselves in a heavy metal tank strapped onto a truck; its fat green hose became our lifeline—filling and refilling buckets and pots so we could drink, wash off the dust, and water dogs and horses.

But none of us left the cattle drive without feeling the beauty of the desert still greened by stalks of mustard and blued by flax and lupine. And none of us will forget the expansive skies each afternoon that filled with soft clouds in the evening. And the birdsong. Then the silence.

Brothers
(In memory of Max Robbins)

YOU NEVER KNOW ABOUT CATTLE DRIVES. Sometimes everyone's real quiet day after day; sometimes the talk is steady and stories come faster than the cattle moving up the road.

It was that way this year with Max and Leo. Max cowboyed for us for years before retiring and now always rides the dusty desert drive with us each year. This time he brought his brother Leo along. And the stories rolled out one after another.

The two started in about the time I collapsed into a folding chair I had dragged out for a nap. I was settled along the small strip of shade from the cow camp trailer—the only shade for 50 miles in any direction in this low-brush landscape.

I'd been up since 4 A.M. working with the others to move the cattle, and now in the warm 3:30 sun the cows and calves were all mothered up and there was not much urgency left to the day.

Just as I was about to drift off, I realized the two men had pulled their chairs next to me. The brothers were somewhere between sixty-five and seventy-five years old but it was hard to tell which was the older. Max started braiding bright yellow baling twine to make a popper for Leo's whip while Leo held the braided end of the twine stretched tight.

They began. "'Member when George died? Died of emphysema. They got to fighting over how to divide up the money so they got them a lawyer and guess who got the biggest share in the end?"

"Did you hear about that Black Angus breeder in Canada that got murdered? That's some story."

"Don't think I heard that."

"No? Well one night that poor sucker went down to check his calves and several days later they found him dead. Buried in the manure. Was only fifty-two."

"Oh yeah, I did hear 'bout that."

"They figured his hired man done it but that breeder was paying big money to drug men, and now they're saying the hired hand took the rap for someone else." Silence.

"Why don't you guys take a nap?" I asked.

"Nope," Max said. "If I sleep during the day, I can't sleep at night."

About that time I gave up the nap idea and headed into the cow camp to begin dinner, carrying their words with me. "Rode thirty-two bucking horses and only one throwed him. He was a double in a movie once. Got $45,000 for it."

By dinnertime, if there had been a lull in the conversation, I had missed it. At the table the two got to spoofing their family. "There were eleven kids in our family," Max told us. Leo nodded. "My mother set twelve places and after she and Dad set down, we'd all scramble to see who got to eat."

"I remember our mother made pancakes a lot," Leo took up. "One time there was one pancake left on the plate and the kerosene lamp went out. When it was lighted again there were twelve forks stuck in my father's hand."

After dinner the crew moved outside the small cow camp to sit in the evening light.

"Has anyone seen my binoculars?" I heard someone ask. "I once lost a pair of binoculars," Max answered. "Never did find them again." And then Leo: "I lost a pair once too, but about a week later . . ." On and on. They never missed a beat, these two brothers with a lifetime of stories, a lifetime of memories out here in the desert.

Jimmy

I AM INTRIGUED BY THE LAND. It is what holds me to our ranch 24 dirt-road miles from town. But this spring I saw the land in a new light. I saw it through Jimmy's eyes.

Jimmy is the man who takes care of the rose gardens in the park that surrounds the East Coast house where I was raised. My husband and I were home for my dad's eightieth birthday, and the first morning, I joined my father in his daily 3-mile walk through this park.

The vast expanse of land, owned by the town, runs from the Connecticut Thruway several miles south to the Long Island Sound. The park is a place to lose yourself. There are woods and hillsides of rock outcroppings and flowering rhododendron, isolated paths that cross grassy knolls, ponds with ducks and small bridges leading to tiny islands. As we walked under dogwood trees in full bloom, my dad and I caught up on our lives.

"There's Jimmy," he interrupted pointing to a slight man, a gardener, snipping leaves off rosebushes not yet in bloom but grouped like sentinels in rows across the wide lawn.

Jimmy stood up when he saw us coming, a wide grin spreading across his face, his olive Italian skin already tinted a light nut-brown by spring sunshine. "Hi there, Mr. Josephy," he called out.

My dad introduced us, first telling me that Jimmy was a good friend who kept an eye on the house when my parents were away. Jimmy nodded thoughtfully. Then my dad began to tell him about my life, explaining, "She lives on a sheep and cattle ranch in Idaho with her husband." Jimmy stepped back in amazement. "No!" he said slowly, the ideas gathering as he spoke. "God's own country! It must be somethin' where you live—on all that land. I love the land."

With a sweeping motion he brought us completely into his garden space.

"I've been working here since 1951, taking care of this park, these roses. I don't use no chemicals like the new guys. And I don't trim the beds that far back," he said, pointing with disdain at the edge around a cluster of roses. "I know this land, you bet, after all these years. I love the quiet. I love the place."

Then he smiled broadly again. "But you should see my garden at home. I got it all planted now, Mr. Josephy," he said, as if my father were awaiting this report. "My tomatoes are in, my basil, broccoli, cabbage, cauliflower." He stopped. "Cauliflower's this big already." Jimmy held one hand 12 inches above the other.

"My garden's big. You could put three apartment units in the space," which meant that in this real estate–booming community his garden plot was valuable property. "But you, now you really got somethin' living out in Idaho."

The next day I was surprised when Jimmy showed up at our door. "I was wondering," he asked hesitantly, "could I meet the cowboy?" I laughed and went to get my husband. For the next twenty minutes the two men talked about the land and "doing God's work," as Jimmy called it.

They walked around Jimmy's three-wheeler parked in front of our house. The cart attached to the back was full of rakes, hoes, and rose clippings. They studied the vehicle, concluding it might ride just a little too close to the road for ranch work.

I asked Jimmy if he had ever been to Idaho. "No," he said, he hadn't been any farther west than the Great Lakes. But still he knew. He had come to meet a "cowboy," another man who was made whole by the feel of soil between his fingers and its musty smell after a rain. Another man who survived best in the quiet and the uncluttered space the land provides.

And now they stood together, sharing the day. Two men: Jimmy with his rose gardens on one side of this sprawling country, and my husband, mountain ranges, prairies, and deserts away. Two men tied inextricably to the land they love.

Summer

IN THIS SEASON the world is swollen with promise. It rustles through grasses grown tall and swaying in the afternoon wind. It shines from leaves of trees that reflect back sunshine onto meadows and brush around them. The world is exuberant, opulent. Flowers flow from the earth, crops reach to the sky, animals fatten and become lazy to the humming of insects.

Birthdays

I HAVE ALWAYS HONORED MY BIRTHDAY, carefully planning hours of self-indulgence. So you can imagine my surprise when, after only two weeks of ranch life and still smacking of city ways, I was asked by my friend to help work his calves.

"It's my birthday," I reminded him solemnly. I was reading a good book at the time. He looked astonished. I quietly, if somewhat petulantly, followed him from the house.

At the corrals, in the safety of his three best cowboys, he explained my options. "There are four things you can do," he began.

"Tag them." I cringed at the thought of shooting plastic colored tags into their drooping ears. I hadn't much enjoyed piercing my own. "Vaccinate them," he continued. I winced. Who in their right mind likes to get or give shots?

"Brand them," he offered. I reeled. The stench of burning hair had already made me dizzy when I first got out of the pickup. I wanted no part of that odious project.

I clung to the promise of the fourth option. "Or you could castrate them," he offered. Silence.

Here it was my birthday and I was about to pass out cold on the ground. I grabbed a fence post for support. "Could you go through that list again?" I asked weakly.

It was a sad day for cowboying. But in the end I could whip that serum into those young calves slick as you please. At least, I reasoned, I was doing something to make them healthy.

But there was one moment of crisis when my friend came over to watch. Squish, an air bubble forced serum out around the base of the needle. My first mistake and he was there watching.

"Diane, if you don't get the medicine in them, these calves might die," he admonished. I was distraught. What if I were responsible for the death of a calf—on my birthday?

I couldn't sleep for nights and checked the calves each day until I was sure they had all survived. Now that I know celebrating birthdays means different things to different people, I carefully plan those days, filling in the calendar well in advance to remind my friend, now my husband, to work the calves another day. It's safer for all of us that way.

24 Miles from Town

WHEN I FIRST HEARD that the highway crew planned to pave part of the dirt road that leads from Carey to our ranch, I was outraged. Pave my road? Invade my solitude? Disturb part of the rough pockmarked highway that runs through pastures, and aspen groves, and along the Little Wood River? Pave the road and people the quiet?

I saw, in my mind, the rutted highway from home to town—the backroad access for hunters and anglers wending their way to streams and the brush-covered foothills of the Pioneer Mountains. The image suddenly erupted into the Hollywood Freeway. I pictured the pot holes smoothed black in one long strip, the pavement gilded with cautionary lines that pierced the vastness in an unending scar. Billboards crowded its edges. Cars, pickups, buses, and trucks crawled bumper to bumper through the open space, breaking the silence with their horns. Beyond the edge of the blacktop in all directions, cattle grazed mindlessly.

"They are going to connect about six miles to the paved area north of town," my husband said.

"No," I wailed. "There will be more people."

He smiled at this response from a woman who, not so long ago, was surrounded by urban conveniences, people, and events. Who only a few years ago had been stunned to find herself staring wide-eyed into a strange new silence. Who once despaired at the sight of her first flat tire in sage-scented isolation. That same woman now was lamenting the loss of 6 miles of dirt road.

I saw pride in his face. I belonged here now, but at what price? Although there would still be a dirt road buffer of 18 miles between "them and us," I was threatened and I feared for our solitude.

There was a time when I would have delighted in a paved road. That was when every trip to town brought the terrible anxiety of a flat tire and a very long walk for help, with rattlers and who knows what else tagging along out of meanness.

So I learned to change a tire with speed, skill, and with jeans and tennis shoes always ready in the car. Flats generally happen when I'm dressed up— that's a given. I never worry about privacy as I change into these work clothes because no one who can help ever comes along until I've tightened the last lug nut—that's also a given.

Recently a neighbor stopped her car to join fifteen steers watching me replace a tire. "I've lived up here twenty-five years," she said as I jammed the well-worn spare into place, "but I've never learned to do that. You're really good," she added as she drove off, leaving me in the dust.

And I am good. Recently when I broke down on Idaho Highway 20 near Mountain Home, three cars raced right by, their drivers waving. "You're doing great," one called out.

But I never would have survived without advice from our son, who saved me with something he learned in a high school shop class. It may be the single most important piece of information I've ever received.

It was this: lefty loosey, righty tighty. Left to loosen, right to tighten. Critical for quick removal of lug nuts 24 miles from town. Lefty loosey, righty tighty. And it works in any number of situations.

If my best friend had this information, she might still visit me despite her three flat tires.

But then again, I really don't need company when I can wander down our dirt road, feel the wind over me, and smell the sweet sagebrush. Or stand in an open field listening to the sandhill cranes and watch the last traces of sun wash the buttes with stark white light before releasing the day into darkness.

Today there are still 18 miles of washboard silence, and I'll fight to keep it that way.

The Wedding

THE BOUNDARIES OF TOLERANCE in families are a mystery to me. Sometimes its members complain at the slightest inconvenience, then withstand amazing hardships without flinching. It was like that with my mother, who never got over the shock that I moved to Alaska in the 1970s, "that wilderness outpost," she moaned every time she called.

I finally decided that only a trip to the forty-ninth state would dispel her morose thoughts. Several days in Anchorage, a gourmet dinner at the Top of the Captain Cook Hotel, shopping at Nordstroms, and hobnobbing with several university friends and her fears about my primitive life would be cast to the winds. But the trip never fully turned her around.

Knowing only this much, you can understand my reluctance to tell my mother I was going to make Idaho my home and spend the rest of my life with a man whose ranch was 24 dirt-road miles from town. Tentatively, I invited her to the early July wedding. It had been about six years since I left Alaska. I crossed my fingers and hoped for the best.

To ease her into the experience, I booked my mother and stepfather into a good hotel in Boise and made dinner reservations at an elegant restaurant. They would need a break between the flight from the east and the drive to the ranch.

It was not my fault the plane was four hours late and that there was no place for them to eat when they arrived at midnight. Nor was it my fault that the hotel's plumbing failed and there was no water for a shower that night or the next morning before they left town for the ranch.

But I didn't know this at the time. I was too busy worrying about the three-day downpour that had turned the ranch into a mud hole. We had planned to roast three lambs over an open fire, but at 3 A.M. the morning of the wedding, I easily convinced myself the rain would make a fire impossible. I tossed and turned in bed. Could we butcher three lamb carcasses in enough small pieces to jam them into every oven around the ranch? Were there enough ovens?

But the weather cleared, and by 7 A.M. the meat was basted and had begun its daylong roast thanks to a friend, an elder Scotsman and neighbor who volunteered to handle the job. He sat by the fire all day, maybe 50 yards from the serving tables, a bottle of scotch by his side, entertaining the curious and the thirsty.

Seven A.M. was also the hour the power went out. Instantly the entire ranch was without water, electricity, or refrigeration for the wedding food and wine.

This was my mother's first trip to Idaho. It was her first time on a working ranch. Although she had left urban life for a Virginia farm to marry my stepfather, her new home was more of an estate, an antebellum affair in the heart of hunt country. It never seemed to get muddy at the farm, certainly never on the deeply pebbled pathways that wound between tall hedges of boxwood and through the rose gardens.

She and my stepfather pulled up to our log cabin ranch house at midday in their rental car. The vehicle was covered in mud. We hugged. They smiled and explained that they were dying for a bath. I smiled and informed them that I was too, but we had no water.

As it turned out, the power came on for an hour at 1:00 and we all rushed to clean up. That is, everyone but my husband-to-be, who missed the chance while he and several ranch hands struggled to put up the outdoor tent in case the sunshine turned to rain again, which of course it didn't. He bathed later in the icy creek behind the house just down from where the champagne was chilling.

We hooked up an old generator and were forced to choose between music and flushing the toilets. It was an easy choice. What's a wedding without music. But then luckily, full power came back late in the afternoon just before we served dinner.

To make amends the next morning I took my parents to the resort community of Sun Valley for lunch. It is where I go for groceries, about 45 miles from the ranch. But I wanted them to feel more comfortable about my new life.

Apparently the trip to town was unnecessary. My mother was unfazed by the hardships of the wedding weekend. And until the day she died, she continued to tell her friends she never understood why her daughter squandered years of her life in a primitive place like . . . Alaska.

Trees

I LOVED THE LANDSCAPE of our ranch from the first moment I saw it. But I confess from the beginning I wondered if the enormous reaches of space filled with rolling hills, sagebrush, and tall grasses couldn't use just a few more trees. Of course, cottonwoods ranged up and down the banks of Friedman Creek, filtering the strong sunshine and catching the breezes to cool our cabin even on the hottest summer afternoons.

But I wondered about just a little more greenness. So I bought my husband an apple tree for our first wedding anniversary, which we planted outside our bedroom window. We watered it and waited for it to grow.

The next fall, I signed up for the Soil Conservation Service tree program and the following spring collected twenty-five fragile seedlings each just shy of a foot tall from the agency office.

I planted the tiny spruce and pine in a field along the side of the house, aspens along the dirt road to our front yard, and lilacs near the cabin doors. Then the struggle began.

For the rest of the summer I watered constantly, dragging hoses for miles from one sprout to another. I was a slave to the seedlings. I turned down lunch invitations in town, convinced the trees would die without constant watering. I cooked quick meals that fit between watering cycles. I read books, with so many interruptions to move hoses that I can't remember what the stories were about.

By midsummer I had to mark the tiny seedlings to keep them from getting lost in the tall grasses. In October I cheered the arrival of early winter and the end of watering.

The next spring, there was no trace of the aspen twigs—gone with the snows as if they had never existed. The lilacs, spruce, and pines barely clung to life. The apple tree was even smaller than I remembered it.

I began my second summer of servitude to this project. After a flurry of spring growth that added several inches to each plant—just enough to give me a false sense of hope—the seedlings settled back to suck up the water and languish in the sun.

The cycle continued. There were losses each winter and long summer days of watering. Now, years later, only three spruces and two lilacs have survived the seasons, the drought, the ranch trucks that have backed over them, and the horses and wild game that have nibbled the tops flat. The healthiest is maybe 2 feet high, and I have lost almost all interest in them.

Only our apple tree is a triumph. After eight years it suddenly blossomed and now gives us fruit. My husband and I fawn over it.

So I gave up on my grove. And simultaneously I stopped clearing the area of cottonwood sprouts from seeds carried to the field by the winds. It was then I realized that these seedlings, without any special attention, were growing into respectable cottonwoods. Now I ponder the word indigenous. Perhaps, I reason, spruce trees would have looked a little strange in this field of tall grasses and wildness where cottonwoods have come to flourish.

Sage Is for Remembering

UTE STEPPED OFF THE AIRPLANE in Idaho directly from her home in Germany. She was a young woman of twenty with a lovely, gentle face, her blond hair in a single braid down her back. She was tall, willowy, and as inquisitive and eager as I remembered her from two years earlier when I stayed with her family in Oldenburg near the North Sea.

She had traveled for twenty-four hours to reach this place and was suspended between exhaustion and wide-eyed wonder. Her first trip alone was so far from home, she admitted in almost perfect English.

The next day, we left for Hailey, where Ute would spend the summer with an American family. She dozed in the car through the summer, desert landscape between Boise and Mountain Home, waking suddenly just after the turnoff to Highway 20.

She sat up and clapped her hands together, looking around at the Bennett Hills and green meadows. "Oh, no," she cried out, laughing and pointing to a field of Hereford cattle. "It's just like in the movies."

I laughed too, suddenly appreciative of this familiar landscape. We talked about the small town of Fairfield when we drove by it, about dry mountain air, farm country, and the sagebrush hillsides beyond.

I told her that I loved the West so much that when I was younger I vacationed here each summer. And every year I returned to my East Coast life dragging large, plastic trash bags of sagebrush. It perfumed my Washington, D.C., home, reminding me there was a landscape beyond the one I inhabited. She asked me if others thought the sage smelled as beautiful as I did. But I couldn't remember.

Outside of the town of Bellevue, I stopped the car. From a bush near the road, I picked several small sprigs of sage for Ute. She smelled them, smiled, nodded, and held them tight.

And in her gesture, I remembered. Others had found the smell as hypnotic as I. Yet I had forgotten. Was it too familiar? The space? The light patterns that marble the hillsides around our ranch? The quiet? The beauty? Perhaps not, so long as there is a sprig of sage for remembering.

The Telephone

THE DUST HAD BARELY SETTLED behind our pickup as we pulled up to our ranch cabin when my mother-in-law drove up beside us.

"Phone's out," she announced proudly, not because it was good news. Precisely the opposite. But there is something satisfying about dumping your frustrations onto someone else, as if to say, "So what are you going to do?"

"It's been out all day," she continued, passing on her insider information. "Tom said he'd report it when he got to town."

Despite my dreams of summer solitude, I was not ready for this kind of isolation until I had cleared away a few more items off my desk. My husband paled. There was too much to do out here to make a half-hour drive to the nearest phone. We were up against deadlines to sell our lambs, our hay, get in touch with repair shops, family. The phone was a necessity.

Yet we probably should have expected this. Losing the phone is one of the principal hazards of ranch life. It happens at least four or five times a summer. One year we lost it every week. "If you get a busy signal for too long, our phone may be down," we advised friends. "Please report it for us." Or this year we say to friends, "If we get cut off, it's our phone. I'll call you right back."

I know when I lift the receiver and hear static, I shouldn't be frustrated. After all, when I first arrived at this isolated ranch, everyone who worked and lived here was on the same line. I learned a lot about this place in those early years. Now we have private lines. And it has been down hill since they were installed.

The phone was brought to the ranch by its original owner years ago when he and his crew strung a single-wire system between bent aspen poles tied to a post set in the ground. Each had an insulator on top.

If a deer hit one, knocking down the glass piece, a ranch hand would simply replace the broken insulator with a beer bottle with the bottom knocked out. If the line drooped, it was strung across a fence post and stapled down. In the winter, if it froze, calls were delayed until midday when temperatures thawed the ice. Then you'd crank up the wall phone and pass the number along to the operator, who knew the whereabouts of everyone in town. "Oh, no, Mary, George just left the office. He's at the Mint Bar. I'll ring for you."

About 1962, when the telephone company wanted to put in a dial system, my husband and our crew did most of the work, replacing the bent aspens with telephone poles and stringing new wires. About twenty years later, the company decided to bury the line. But the wires were left so close to the surface that they were repeatedly damaged by road graders. A good rain washed away the thin layer of dirt, exposing the fragile wires to moisture and knocking out service. Our own private, modern, touchtone phone—useless when it rains hard.

This time, after twenty-four hours without service, my husband and I went to town. We were not in our apartment long when my mother-in-law arrived, clutching her two address books. The phone stayed busy the rest of the morning. When had we become so dependent on this instrument?

That day, I reported the phone out of order at 8 A.M. I spared nothing in my presentation of our crisis and appeared to convince the operator who assured me we were at the top of her emergency list. At 10 A.M. I called again, only to be told they had no record of any previous reports. I raged.

By noon, my husband took up the crusade. "We're working on it," he was assured. He called again. "What do you mean my phone is probably out because of all the rain and flooding?" he barked in frustration. "We're in the middle of a drought. Where are you?" Pause. "St. Paul?"

"St. Paul, Minnesota?" my husband bellowed. "The Mississippi's flooding, but not in Idaho. How can you fix my phone from St. Paul?"

Now, an experience like this can be tough on the heart. But fortunately someone did reconnect the phone, maybe even the operator in St. Paul. We returned home after three days without service.

And the old-timers at the ranch just shook their heads, muttering to each other as they always do knowing the phone would go out soon again and they'd be wagering how long it would take the repairman to arrive while we waited out here isolated in silence.

Guard Dogs

WE RUN SHEEP AND CATTLE on our Idaho ranch, but it's the sheep we fret over. They are the most vulnerable to predators as they graze on winter desert pastures, then move to high mountain ranges north of our ranch headquarters each summer. Sometimes at night I wake to the chilling howl of coyotes and a panic races through me as I fear for the ewes and their lambs in the nearby hills.

To protect these animals we, like many of our neighbors, have begun using guard dogs—large, white Great Pyrenees. Their barking frightens predators, so we have less need for trappers to keep our sheep safe.

We get the Pyrenees as pups just weaned from their mothers, and put them in a large pen near our house with two or three lambs so the animals will bond together. For days we watch from a distance the ritual of lambs and dogs becoming familiar.

In the beginning they stare hard at each other from opposite ends of the pen. But curiosity brings them together, and one day we see the pups curled up against the lambs napping in the shade of a quiet afternoon.

We watch constantly but cannot touch because the dogs must bond to sheep, not people, if they are to guard effectively. Petting would confuse them, and for us that is the hard part because they are irresistible as puppies.

When they are grown, the small bundle of fur is transformed into a great but still lovable huge beast of a white dog who is taken to a band of sheep in the hills with his lamb friends. The herder brings him food each day and the dog lives with his new family, barking fiercely at strange sights and sounds.

The dogs work well until that day when the sheep roam too near a public mountain trail. Then, a well-intended but misguided hiker begins petting the great white dog, thinking he is lost among the sheep. And maybe . . . just a crust of sandwich or some salami because he's so sweet. Who could resist?

Later that night we get a call. "We found a stray dog with your sheep. He followed us down the trail so we brought him home with us."

It is always the same. And always we drive the miles to pick up the dog and take him back to his band, and always he bounds out of the truck when he sees the sheep, at home again in the hills with family.

Pink House

It was impossible to drive by the pink house and not notice it. It sat in the middle of Nevada open space on one of those typically Nevada roads that extends lonely and forever into the distance. The emptiness was broken only occasionally by a ranch house or a trailer sitting back off the highway, battered by the elements.

It was like this with the pink house. But despite the desolate landscape, you couldn't help notice it. It was painted a deep pink—sort of dusty rose—a color that clearly triumphed over its environment. Even the unsightly stack of hay bales toppled and rotting in the front yard could not dim the effect of the bright house with its matching pink wishing well nearby.

I have often noted—sometimes with humor, more often in frustration—this tension between the business of farming and the need for an attractive home in which to live. At our own ranch, visitors must drive past our shop and outbuildings to get to our cabin.

At this working area, one or another ranch truck is settled, hood up, tire off. Nearby are machine parts, a front-end loader for the tractor, a disc, a chisel plow. Gigantic dual tires are propped against the shop wall. Elevated fuel tanks are outlined against the blue sky. It is the way with ranch yards. Pieces of farm machinery scattered around empty spaces. The outdoor sculpture of our lives.

When I first moved to the ranch, I cleaned up with a vengeance, trying to make a home. I tore up strips of grass along the log cabin and planted flowers—daisies, columbines, yarrow, and flax. I painted the trim on the house and the old peeling chairs on the porch. I was making the home beautiful but when I stepped out onto the lawn, I winced at the view of the shop and storage buildings beyond.

The next year, I planted gooseberry and currant bushes and some lilacs along the fence. In time these may block out the jumble of ranch life to the east.

But whenever I'm weeding my garden and swearing and sweating at the work, my husband laughs. "That's why Mrs. Laidlaw never planted flowers," he reminds me.

How often have I heard this disturbing story of the original ranch owners? How Mr. Laidlaw refused to put up a fence and instead let the sheep graze right up to the front door to keep the grass down. My husband also reminds me—every time he has to mow the lawn—how well the Laidlaw plan worked. Then I remind him that Jim Laidlaw barely had the last shovelful of dirt thrown on his grave when his widow put up the fence around the cabin so she could finally create a bit of beauty for herself, free from sheep droppings and ragged range.

Let the men continue to plant and plow, bale and stack, and acquire whatever machinery they need to make the operation pay for itself. Ranch wives will always save the place with a few flowers here, a bush there, and a coat of paint when we can afford it, maybe even dusty rose when we need a really strong antidote.

Skunks

OUR RANCH HOUSE is a rambling collection of three 1880 log cabins. My friends see it as a lazy summer place, with Friedman Creek flowing behind and vast open space beyond the front fence. What they rarely notice are the cracks, crevices, and crawl spaces that come with this old structure, places for all kinds of critters to bring the outdoors in.

At night I often wake to the patter of paws above me in the ceiling. Spiders, flies, and crawling creatures freely explore the cabin. There are small snakes in the garden and mice that scatter nuggets of dry dog food in dark corners around the house. In self defense I have come to ignore these pests if only because I am so badly outnumbered.

But I draw the line at skunks. When I first moved to this ranch, my only experience with these animals was Bambi's sweet friend, Flower. But soon after I arrived, I began to sniff them in corners of the house as they burrowed underneath the cabin.

In disgust I encouraged my husband to rid us of these menaces. His best Marine Corps training snapped into place. Baamm, baamm the weapon resounded, and then the stench hit. My eyes began to burn. Waves of nausea swept over me. The foul smell was everywhere, sneaking and seeping through the house, clinging to objects in its path, including clothing. Days later when I thought the aroma had disappeared, I braved town, but even friends cut a wide swath around me.

That same summer, we awoke one moonlit night to skunk scent. My husband grabbed a weapon and headed outside. I screamed after him "Don't you dare bring him around here. The smell will ruin everything."

In the white light, I saw the hunter chasing the animal across the open fields. But then I looked again. My husband was in full retreat. I shouted furiously, "Don't bring him back here." He yelled back, "You don't understand the problem." And then I saw the skunk in hot pursuit. In an instant the man flung himself through the door and slammed it behind him. Some things just don't go the way you plan.

It was a terrifying night but as a result, our warfare turned defensive. Today, large rocks piled against the foundation of our house form a bunker against these terrorists so they no longer can find crawl space under the cabin for nesting. They have disappeared. It is heaven and we can smell the flowers again.

Old Cabins

THE EMPTY FRAMES of old pioneer log cabins lie scattered across our western landscape. They are clustered along Highway 20 between Fairfield and Arco and settled in pockets across our ranch lands north of Carey. Long abandoned, these structures lean away from the wind, bleached and battered by weather, perhaps one hundred years after their construction.

We cannot drive far into the backcountry without seeing old cabins. Soon after I arrived here, my husband and I made the hard half-hour drive in a pickup over a little-used dirt road to a farmstead with an abandoned barn and cabins flung across the land.

It was an early summer day and we followed Friedman Creek into a deep canyon, then out onto the flat meadows of Shaw Field where the cabins appeared. In the midmorning stillness, we prowled from one building to another, all empty shells with gaping holes where doors and windows once blocked fierce weather. Today they are a quiet reminder of dreams that did not fit the landscape.

On another day we took the same road up Friedman Creek even farther into the draw to check some cows. There, in the wildness, were more cabins almost lost in the tall and reckless grasses pushing against the logs. This small settlement seemed lonelier—perhaps because of the small, struggling orchard at this site, planted long ago when life must have seemed somehow permanent to this family.

Once, I returned to Alaska, a place of far-flung, remote villages, for an economic development conference. I listened to panelists discuss the plight of Alaska Natives who live on the barest income miles from urban centers. These settlements, whether strung along the Nenana River or clinging to the edge of the Chuckchi Sea, have only the faintest interest in the twenty-first century.

Today, these people live off the land as they have throughout history, despite congressional attempts in the early 1970s to coax Alaska Natives into western economic business ventures for their collective livelihoods.

"There are no job opportunities out there," a non-native economist complained to conference participants. "Maybe we should move the people to the jobs," a second speaker added, brushing aside the violent displacement this would involve. And in that meeting room, I thought of the abandoned homesites around our ranch.

How different it was for pioneers to build and move on—to start again and again in pursuit of a dream. They were a people on the move, anyway. But today it is not the same for these Alaska Native people or for the families living in our rural towns scattered throughout the West.

They are people of the land—all of them. People who understand the meaning of home and know themselves best living off familiar resources. And if we don't listen to stories of our landscape, many of these families will be lost, and with them a lifetime of learning the secrets of this country.

Shoshone

IT WAS ON THE EVENING NEWS this week. I had been expecting it, dreading it, and I winced when I heard it alone in my car. After seven years, the drought that has sucked the life out of southern Idaho has begun to exact its final price.

The story came out of Lincoln County, the small farming region between Twin Falls and Sun Valley, between Gooding and Rupert, in the south-central part of the state. There, the Farmers Home Administration announced, it will send out its first farm foreclosures—two dozen the story said—to families who have had so few crops, so little water, they cannot repay loans made during better days. Each foreclosure letter, in each mailbox, strikes at the heart of small-town Idaho. There would be twenty-four this time. Twenty-four in this rural county of fewer than 250 full-time farmers.

I remember the panic in the countryside several years ago and the strain on friends and neighbors as crop prices plummeted and bankers became impatient. There has been a break in time since those days, but not in the fear farmers carry around with them. They stand outside each morning squinting into brilliant blue skies wishing for a hint of gray. I know, because from my ranch house porch, I search the horizon too.

Last spring I walked the desert country of Lincoln County before we moved our cattle through the area. The parched earth was already kicking up dust devils where there should have been ponds of snowmelt.

Many of these farmers were lucky to have water until early June, the county agent tells me sadly. "Nineteen eighty-six was the last year water ran into September," he adds.

It seems particularly hard to have this happen in Lincoln County, with communities like Richfield, Dietrich, and Shoshone that have doggedly fought to save themselves. I have seen its people come together to hold their fiddler festivals, local art gatherings, Iron Horse roundup, parades, and rodeos—events that might bring visitors into their communities.

I cheered with the town when Shoshone high school juniors and seniors met each afternoon to plot the future of their county, then traveled to the state capital with plans and charts to show Department of Commerce officials. They were marketing their future, "so we won't have to leave home to find work," one was quoted in the newspaper.

The people of Lincoln County are persistent and proud. But their land is cracked and dry and their reservoir is dangerously low. Their fields are tired and in need of new seed. Now their families watch the sky waiting for rain. And they wait for the mail hoping there is no foreclosure notice, but they know time is running out.

Grand Champion

IN THE 4-H SHEDS at the county fair, dirt is the only floor around. It kicks up dry and dusty and creeps into the eyelets of shoes. That's just for starters. There'll be sawdust and probably sheep and cattle droppings before it's over. This is why most everyone is in cowboy boots.

This is the county fair, and whether it's the town of Carey or Cascade, it feels like any other. And although you've checked out the prize cucumbers and pies, oil paintings and crochet pieces, you are really here to wander through the sheds of freshly washed and brushed young animals—lambs, steers, hogs, rabbits, chickens—sizing them up, anticipating the ribbon winners.

Chances are you're too hot to worry about your feet anyway, and you'll end up drinking too many sticky sweet drinks as if they could protect you from the fierce sunshine.

The animal judging always takes place during the hottest part of the day. It is the anxious time when kids face the moment they've worked for all summer. Freshly scrubbed, hair slicked back, cowboy shirt ironed, nervous youngsters parade their prize pets in front of the experts in a makeshift ring. Mothers, brothers, and sisters fan themselves vigorously with their programs. Fathers nod seriously when their kids pass in front of them. Everyone is buzzing and pointing.

Then an animal refuses to move. There are words. You hold your breath for this child and you mutter at the animal who can ruin months of work with too much stubbornness.

Suddenly they are down to six finalists—say, lambs. The kids hold tight to the small heads to keep their animals still while their own faces flash pride, hope, and terror all at once.

The judges circle again. Parents who have fidgeted and kicked at the dust over the last ten minutes stand rigid. Mothers stop fanning themselves. Brothers and sisters no longer push each other. Flies hover brazenly. Everyone is standing on tiptoes for a better look.

The judge writes down a few notes, then speaks into his microphone. "Let's give these kids and their good-looking animals a big hand," he suggests. He talks about hard work and pride.

"And now for the grand champion," he announces getting right to the issue. "Number 12, a fine Suffolk lamb owned by April Witten." All eyes move to the young girl in the ring whose face is now in full grin, but she does not lose her composure. She has been trained to handle the moment. Applause. Next the reserve grand champion is announced. More applause.

Then April, with her blond hair pulled into a single tight braid, a rose-colored cowboy shirt tucked into stiff new jeans, begins to circle the arena with her champion lamb. She is followed by an older boy pulling at the reserve champion and smiling broadly.

Then, as quickly as it assembled, the crowd disperses. Participants congratulate the winners. Others get a pat on the shoulder and the ever-present reminder: "Next year, next year." You hear it everywhere around the room—the well-worn anthem of the farmer, learned here in the early years. Maybe next year.

4-H Sale

THE TWELVE-YEAR-OLD GIRL pushes her prize steer to the center of the outdoor ring. He doesn't stop so she runs around to head him off from the front, placing her body directly in his path. Dust kicks up around the two of them. He turns, and she turns with him. The dance continues while the auctioneer begins his banter into a tinny microphone. He is set up in the back of a shiny red pickup pulled against the inside of the outdoor ring. He is leaning with one leg resting on the tailgate, looking neighborly.

"Here's a fine animal, folks," he calls out. "Hang on, Cindy, you're doing great," he coaches the exasperated young girl fixed on slowing down 1,000-plus pounds of animal. The steer itself looks confused and finally stops at the far end of the dusty arena.

"Can you bring 'em out here so we can all get a look?" the auctioneer asks tentatively. After all, Cindy is there to sell her animal—this beautiful brown and white hulk of a Hereford that only yesterday was selected grand champion. The buyers need a look at the goods. Or do they?

This is a 4-H livestock sale, after all, where all the rules of smart buying are broken with the first bid. As a matter of fact, if any of the tough-looking men sitting in the small grandstands or hanging over the fence in the hot sunshine bought cattle for their own ranching operations the way they will buy today, they would be out of business in no time. But then this is kind of a family, kind of a community, affair after all.

The first bid comes from Cindy's grandpa. It's high. The branch manager of the local bank, out for a little goodwill, counters with an offer. Then the grandfather, then the owner of the local independent grocery store. By now the grandfather is feeling pretty confident and bids up the steer again, countered by the bank manager and the grocer, then Catapult Farms.

"This is the grand champion, folks," the auctioneer reminds the rows of parents and local business leaders. But by now the animal is already bringing in a dizzying price.

Cindy has just struck it rich. She stands in the center ring stroking the belly of the Hereford with her long cattle prod, trying to look nonchalant while her mind is racing to count the money. The Grand Champion goes to the bank manager. "Let's have a big hand for First Savings Bank on Main Street." People in the stands stop fanning themselves long enough to applaud and pick up the large cup at their feet for a sip of soft drink, now mostly melted ice.

Cindy leads her steer out of the ring and the reserve champion and its young owner enter. The circling and the bidding start again. It is exactly the same. A proud relative leads off, a merchant in the community takes over, and the animal nets big money for its small owner. It takes the sting out of the sale for one child after another all afternoon. And grand champion or not, all the livestock sell this way.

There will be pictures of youngsters with the bank manager, the owners of the grocery store, the feed store, the newspaper, several livestock outfits, that later will be mounted on respective business walls. Then, once again, generous merchants and proud kids will strut like heroes in the community for yet another year.

Free Marketplace

WHEN WE MOVE CATTLE across the desert, I ride our horse Charro, sinking into the rhythm of his walk as he ambles behind the cows and calves. We are absorbed in the movements of the livestock, of a cow drifting to the right or a calf to the left to find new grasses. Slowly Charro walks toward the stray, our movement enough to send the animal back to the long line of livestock strung down the desert road. There is no world but this one, this day.

It is the same when we farm. Hours go by on the tractor and we are absorbed in turning winter ground, making it ready for seed, moving up and down the field in a straight line. We watch the stubble and grasses in front of the machine turn into chocolate-brown chunks of earth behind us. Hours go by.

It is no wonder, with our lives so full of the outdoors, that when the keynote speaker began to talk about the concentration of power in the food industry, farmers and ranchers in the meeting room squinted as if the sun were shining in their eyes. The ideas were difficult to understand. We raise our commodities and hope for better prices so we can make it until the next year. What do we really know about the buyers, the markets?

The speaker was a professor from the University of Missouri come to Idaho for this farm conference. "There aren't any small packers anymore," he began, referring to the livestock industry. "They've been forced out. Notice how often the names appear and reappear."

We looked at the handout in front of us. Largest beef packers—first, Iowa Beef Processors (IBP); second, ConAgra; third, Cargill. Largest pork packers—IBP, ConAgra, Cargill. Turkeys—ConAgra, Rocco Turkeys. Broilers—Tyson Foods, ConAgra. Lamb—ConAgra, Superior Packing. Flour milling—ConAgra, Archer Daniels Midland, then Cargill. "Notice how the names appear and reappear," he said again.

He continued, "The problem used to be monopolies. A company would control 90 percent of a market. Now there are oligopolies—several companies control 20 percent each of all the markets. New ways to concentrate power. It's legal unless you can prove collusion," he added.

"And these companies aren't just setting the price on your cattle and lambs." He flashed a picture of a grocery bag with products sticking out of the top—things I've bought—Hunt's Ketchup, Wesson Oil, Peter Pan Peanut Butter, Orville Reddenbacher Popcorn, Healthy Choice Soup, Butterball Turkeys. "All owned by ConAgra," he announced. "And then there is Cargill, but that's another story."

I thought about the words of writer Wendell Berry, who told a gathering of farmers that when people stop caring about quality, the family farmer will be lost.

In less than an hour, I saw it all—documented and footnoted in academic and government reports. While we have been herding cattle and turning the earth, the revered free marketplace has become the playground of ConAgra, Cargill, IBP, Tyson Foods, and others.

For the consumer this means tasteless, factory-produced food doctored for long shelf life. For those of us on the land without local meatpacking plants, this means we have no bargaining power. Now, as I ride the ridges and meadows of our ranch, I know to look over my shoulder, no longer trusting the easy silence around me.

Rain

I COULDN'T HELP MYSELF. It was as if I were possessed by some demon as I pressed my foot harder and harder on the gas pedal. Stones and rocks from the dirt road flew up banging the car as they hit, and still I wanted to go faster.

My eyes moved from the road to the rearview mirror looking for the terrible choking dust that would coat the back of the car. The gritty dust that had become the ominous sign of drought along with burned grasses, empty lakebeds, withered hay crops. But now, as fast as I could go, I could raise nothing behind me.

The change began two days ago with a brief rain, our first sign of hope in months. Afterward we had gone to a neighbor's corral in the early evening to see his sheep. It was sweater-cool after months of unusual heat.

The rancher, his wife, and their Basque herder were putting the last animals in the pens for the lamb shipping the next morning. The sky was full of evening colors. We talked anxiously about the lambs and estimated their weights. This rancher was the first producer to ship this year.

He fretted over the poor spring feed caused by drought. The dogs ran excitedly around us. The herder's horse, who often confused himself for a human, hovered over our shoulders as if to listen to our words. We stood in the tall grasses and looked out over cottonwoods, aspen, and soft rolling foothills. In the stillness of late day a sense of hope settled over us.

The next evening we heard the news. The lambs had weighed only 109 pounds—light for lambs that should weigh close to 125. The effects of the drought.

That same evening it rained again. My husband and I stood in our yard, feeling the moisture on our dry skin, and hugged each other. It continued off and on through the night and I awoke several times feeling a new calm from its soft patter on the roof. It rained lightly when I left for our own lamb shipping the next morning, and I drove with reckless abandon.

Faster and faster and still no dust. It was joyous. And when I heard the men at the corrals worrying that the road to town would be too slippery for the livestock trucks, I could only laugh. What better news than muddy roads at last.

Beavers

I OFTEN WONDER at humankind's erratic response to wild things. One day we honor the prowess of an animal, and the next we try to destroy it as a predator. This is true for large and small creatures alike. Think of the beaver. Certainly no animal has suffered from human inconsistency more than these funny, furry, bucktoothed creatures who over the years have been treated as victim, villain, and now savior.

The first white men to reach the New World almost trapped the animal out of existence for its prized pelt. Later, farmers trying to irrigate arid lands went after these natural dam-builders who rechanneled precious water away from crops.

But today these same skills are earning new respect for the beaver. If allowed to build their dams, water ponds up in previously dry areas, healing eroded streambanks and turning sagebrush flats into green meadows. And so in the West, some ranchers are bringing beavers back to their lands.

Beavers have flourished on our place for years. On trips into seldom-seen corners of backcountry we see a beaver's work along a lazy stretch of river. Tangled branch lodges, still ponds, and felled aspen trees create pools of water that turn the surrounding landscape green.

We rarely see beavers at work because they are nocturnal animals and usually afraid of people. So you can imagine how surprised my husband and son were several years ago to see a brazen beaver swim right up to them when they were fishing in an isolated rocky river canyon. It stared hard as if to say, "Whoever you are, this is my river."

Only moments before, my husband had pointed out the animal. "Be quiet, let's watch him," he suggested, never expecting a confrontation. But this animal was more concerned about his river than he was afraid of strangers. Vigorously he smacked his tail against the water, showering the two fishermen onshore.

Quickly reassessing their plans, father and son decided to try another pool downriver and leave the beaver his territory. But no sooner had a line floated onto the water than their challenger was back. They moved again, this time past a rocky stretch in the river made almost impassable by tangled brush.

But within moments there was loud thrashing and crashing through the barricade. The fishermen were so curious about this persistent creature that they climbed out onto a large boulder in the middle of the stream for a better look, only to watch the animal break through the snag to charge them. The beaver swam frenetically around and around the rock, trying to get at these trespassers.

"Now, we weren't trapped or forced out," the two fishermen insisted as they explained their early departure. "But it was getting late after all and well . . . it was quite a ways back to the truck."

Today we laugh at the story of the beaver who saved his river. And with each retelling, we honor the isolated places around our home where some animals have never seen humans and have no fear of them, places where wildness still can exist and even surprise us on an afternoon fishing trip.

Birds

IT IS USUALLY QUIET at our cabin. Any sound that comes along is no more serious than a soft afternoon wind brushing through the cottonwoods behind the house, or gentle birdsong now and then from the nearby willows.

But this year, birds from out of nowhere fill the trees and rock the silence with frenzied screeching. They are not the quiet, small birds of past years but seem larger and highly agitated.

I suspect most of them are the beautiful black and white magpie, a predator that shrieks angrily into the world around it. Whatever the birds might be, their presence adds a new shrillness to the quiet space around me.

Twice recently, they have awakened me with chilling cries from trees near my bedroom window. I lunge into the early-morning light, dreading the sight of feathers flying and small birds spinning downward from high branches to a violent death. But I see nothing. The squawking and screeching continue even while I peer into the dark interior of the towering spruce outside my door.

Throughout the day, I hear the same terrifying commotion from a tree behind the house or one on the other side of the yard. Why this year? I wonder. Why this sudden melodrama? Will the birds frighten each other away so that next year there will be only emptiness and quiet? Or will they grow in numbers and noise, battling each other until only the strongest remain?

I know part of the problem is that there are so few trees around our ranch. Most of the land is open space, sagebrush foothills, and chains of green willows along meadow streams. Much of this cacophony may come from the numbers of birds seeking a place to nest among so few cottonwoods and spruce around our log cabin.

There is a sale notice on our kitchen table. It is an ad for a neighbor's remote ranch. He can no longer afford to farm his land. He is defeated, resigned to losing his 800 acres. We don't see him in town much anymore.

In bold letters on this simple flyer, real estate promoters have laid out their plans: "A chance for a ranch of your own. Twenty-acre parcels permitted." I realize that our remote landscape may soon fill with people.

This year the birds come in alarming numbers, violating their own space, crowding each other recklessly. And it seems we are not so very different from these winged creatures.

The Knoll

"WHAT'S THAT ON THE HILLTOP?" visitors to our remote ranch ask almost immediately after they arrive. They point to the gravesite of stacked rocks on the butte across from our cabin. You can see the perfectly rounded hill and the monument at its crown for miles.

In the pale light of early evening we round up guests, climb into the pickup, the hardier ones in the back, and head for the winding road to the knoll. The truck, even in four-wheel-drive, pulls hard up the deeply rutted, steep incline until it heaves over the last rise and eases across the ridge, stopping in front of the monument of stacked rock enclosed by a peeling log fence.

There my husband begins his tale. "This is the resting place of Old Man Laidlaw who founded this ranch," he explains. "Jim Laidlaw was a remarkable man, a Scotsman and a sheep man who brought the first Suffolk bucks to the United States. He introduced the first Angus cattle to the area in the early part of the century."

As I listen to this familiar tale, I am struck by the breathtaking view from this high place and its similarity to the many pictures I've seen of Scotland. It must have been part of the appeal for Jim Laidlaw.

The story goes that he had a friend, named Jim Teleford, who lived 8 miles across the hills. Every so often, one or the other walked the distance through the backcountry to visit his friend. For the rest of the day and evening they drank a fifth of good scotch together and played cards. The next day, the neighbor walked home.

They made a pact. When the first one died, the other would bring a case of Johnny Walker Black Label to the wake to bury with the body.

Laidlaw died first, in midwinter. In his will he directed his family to bury him on this knoll that looks out over the ranch, but the ground was frozen hard. So they put him in cold storage in Boise until spring. When they went to bury him, they found the knoll was solid rock, so they had to dynamite a place for the casket.

The wake began and Teleford, good to his word, showed up with the case of Johnny Walker scotch. Of course, the mourners decided there was nothing to do but have one last drink in honor of the deceased. So they broke open the case and passed a bottle around. Then another and another.

My husband explains, "Somewhere, we think there is a bottle or two of scotch buried at this site, then . . . maybe not. But that's not the end of the story."

He continues, "Several years later when Mrs. Laidlaw died, they realized they had forgotten to blast a hole big enough for two when they buried her husband. More dynamite would blow Jim out of the ground. So today her remains lie next to him in a small urn, probably somewhere near the Black Label."

Every year the Laidlaw family members visit the knoll to remember their parents. My husband and I can understand Jim Laidlaw's attachment to this site. The knoll is our favorite view too.

From here the ranch takes on a completeness as I scan its wildness from the Pioneer mountain peaks in the east to the string of ridge lines against the horizon in the west. From this place, I can see cattle and sheep grazing on pastures and patterns of crops, bright green and yellow in the afternoon sun. All of it, the wildness and the work, is the design of our lives.

And I never visit this place without remembering the rich history of the ranch, its quiet message of endurance and survival, and without laughing at the story of our own "buried treasure."

Lamb Shippings

EVERY YEAR IN JULY AND AUGUST, we ship fat lambs to market in the 5 A.M. stillness. We have the world to ourselves as we drive to the corrals over mountain backroads through aspen groves and along streams that keep the Pioneer mountain meadows green, even in drought years.

Friends and family gather inside the small sheepherder's camp waiting for daylight. We tame the morning chill with cups of strong black coffee warmed on the small woodstove in the herder's wagon. The Coleman lantern casts shadows over those of us huddled inside. The old-timers swap stories about lamb prices and the way things used to be.

With the first trace of light we head to the corrals and the waiting trucks. We button jackets and slip on gloves as we go. Herders, sheep men, buyers, truckers, neighbors, family—all scatter through the maze of pens to herd as many as 2,000 animals forward. Children no taller than the sheep jump up and down, clapping mittened hands and shouting "Yip, yip, yip." Excited dogs run back and forth, and the sea of undulating, white wool bodies moves forward.

At the front of the long chute, the buyer and Denny, our sheep manager, open and close small hinged panels as the sheep pass. When all the panels are flat along the side of the chute, the fat lambs will run the full length of the alley onto the truck. When Denny swings the gate open, it blocks the ewes, forcing them to turn into a large pen to the right. Farther up the chute the buyer swings open another panel if he thinks a lamb is too small to be loaded onto the truck. That animal will veer into the pen to the left of the alley. There he joins other small lambs that will remain behind to graze on ranch pastures until a later shipping.

All this happens in a split second, each man eyeing the animals as they run one on top of another toward the truck, determining instantly whether it goes right, left, or straight ahead.

The loading takes several hours and by the time we've finished, the sun has warmed the day and jackets hang from fence posts. Now we are hot, dusty, and hungry as we head back to camp for baked ham, sweet rolls, breads, juice, and coffee.

But last year in the early-morning chill I was reminded sharply that the old ways are changing. I pulled off the main highway and immediately saw a Winnebago sitting along the side of the road, then a pickup with a camper shell, and a van settled against a rock outcropping. I lost count after ten such vehicles. Each site was littered with lawn chairs, grills, coolers, and dogs. Laundry hung from rope strung between trees. Although these campers were sleeping, their presence broke the stillness.

Sixty years ago, more than 100,000 sheep summered in these mountains. Now the 20,000 that remain are the subject of environmental impact statements. The local community, in pursuit of tourist dollars, frets more about the grass eaten by the remaining sheep than about the tramping of summer visitors. Every year our sheep are forced to travel farther and wider through the hills to avoid new housing developments and populated hiking and camping areas.

Today there is still a 5 A.M. quiet, but I know statistics claim that the footprint of recreation is the second greatest threat, after polluted water, to open space in the West. This morning, the statistics gather in the cluttered campsites I see as I drive the backroads of mountain meadows. And when their numbers become too great, it will be our sheep that will be forced to move on, move higher, move out of sight, to clear the way for the new West.

Summer Storms

EVERY NIGHT FOR A WEEK I have awakened to thunder, lightning, and fierce winds. At first I offered gentle words I didn't fully believe to calm our agitated dog next to the bed. But now I can no longer soothe the frightened animal.

This is the time of year when angry weather wreaks havoc across the landscape and there is only restless sleep. Each morning, I wake to smell the air then look anxiously out the window for plumes of smoke. When I find no telltale signs of fire, I fall back relieved that we've made it through another night.

But the land is a fire hazard. Despite our 6,000-foot ranch elevation, grasses dry out and turn brown in August. And I am reminded of my own brush with fire several years ago. My husband and I scrambled to put out a small blaze we spotted in a field on our way to town. I frantically beat at the patch of flames with a jacket while he threw shovels of dirt into them. But we could not get the best of the fire until more help came along.

I will always remember two things about that effort: the panic when I realized the flames were spreading so fast that two people could not match their speed, and the intense heat of the fire. It choked air from my lungs and I suddenly understood the terror of the word inferno. It had seemed such a small fire but we had almost lost it. It was then I learned a new respect for these summer outbursts.

So recently, when I found a note from my husband about a blaze in one of our fields, I was frightened. "I've gone to check," he wrote. I scanned the skies for smoke as I drove to the site he had described. When I got there, I saw no fire but only two chartreuse BLM fire trucks parked on the rim. The crew was packing up, but they pointed across the river to the ridge line where there had been flames. "It's out," they told me. And I took my first full breath of air since I had left the house.

We had avoided fire this time, but we had not made it through the night unscathed. Several hours later, Denny brought the grim news that fifty-one of our ewe lambs and two large bucks had been struck by lightning. We found the bodies on their sides, toppled by the force of nature, rigid yet huddled together still as they must have been when they were standing. It was a freak occurrence. They were not in a high place or near trees, but in a green alfalfa field gathered for comfort against the bellicose summer storm. In this solace they shared death.

Days later I still reel at the memory of the sheep, again stunned by the pain and loss that are the constant counterpoint to this beautiful landscape. And now at the flash of lightning, the rumble of thunder, I hide under sheets as I did when I was young. I no longer have words to calm our anxious dog.

Carey

I DRIVE THROUGH the small southern Idaho town of Carey almost every day. I stop for the mail at the post office on Main Street just across from the Mormon church, then drive past the fair grounds, turning left toward the Little Wood River Reservoir. From the edge of town, the road winds through stretches of green farm country and then into open pastureland. Even though our ranch headquarters is 24 miles down this road, Carey is our hometown.

It remains today, as it was, even before the farm crisis of the 1980s, small, underserviced, in need of a coat of paint, stranded on the edge of the sagebrush desert on Highway 20. It is almost 25 miles in any direction from a neighboring town not much bigger than itself. Carey is a long-distance call to anywhere beyond its last farmhouse.

People driving through for the first time are surprised to see some of its storefronts boarded up and tall weeds spilling across empty lots. They're not familiar with rural America. When they pull into town, they often look past the shell of an old gas station, never seeing its sun-bleached words, "Gas for Less," on the side of the deserted building.

They miss the Sports Shop surrounded by dusty pickups parked haphazardly. They never go in for coffee, never pull up a chair with the six or seven men, local farmers and sheep ranchers, talking farm prices. They never scan the sepia-toned walls and wooden cabinets or pull open the humming coolers for the store's offerings. And there is a smattering of everything: shotgun shells, horseshoes, movie videos, beer, ice cream, milk, and the daily paper. Most travelers head somewhere else rather than check into the seldom-used, four-unit Carey Motel, formerly called "The Paris." It belongs to the Sports Shop owner too.

Across the street they may see Adamson's General Store, long on canned items, short on fresh foods. At its gas station every summer, hobbled farm trucks wait for flat tires to be repaired while lumbering RVs crowd around its gas pumps. Carey is one of the few stops on the quiet, backroad highway leading east to Idaho Falls and Yellowstone Park.

On the edge of town, several blocks past the turnoff to the school, cars pull up to the imposing log cabin building, the Loading Chute Café. Here the soup and pie are homemade and the coffee is always hot.

Often people tell me that they drove through Carey but they blinked and missed it. They think this is funny. I'm glad they never stopped. They wouldn't think to ask Verda about cooking for the big ranches down the road, or Jim about this year's lamb prices, or Dale about Luke's football game, or Harold about the Laidlaw Park range tour through the springtime desert. These travelers just race through this quiet town without knowing about the summer picnics and rodeos, the harvest dinner, the Christmas pageant.

Carey is a farm town, a working town on the edge of yesterday, only a small break in the sagebrush landscape. Carey is, in fact, rural America.

Cattle Guards

THE LANGUAGE OF RANCHING has become part of my everyday life. So much so that I often forget that familiar words can sound strange to people from town. Everyday words like "cattle guards," for instance.

"What?" a friend interrupted my story.

"A cattle guard. You know," I replied. "No, I don't," she said. I was dumbfounded.

I don't remember when or how I first learned about cattle guards—the metal bars laid inches apart across a shallow ditch in the road. They replace the need for a gate where the road cuts through a fence line and are as effective as barbed wire at keeping livestock in one field and out of another.

Animals' hooves get caught between the metal rungs and they learn at an early age to stay away from these strange traps. Although a seemingly open road may look inviting to a cow bursting with wanderlust, the cattle guard will stop her quickly.

I can understand an animal's fear. Even though my foot is considerably larger than a hoof and would not get stuck between the slats, I always come to a halt at a cattle guard when I'm out walking. Casually, I size it up, trying not to look at the sluggish water below. Then I tiptoe from rung to rung, balancing carefully as if I were on a log suspended above a roaring river. I know that it would take only the slightest misstep for me to be sucked into the stagnant puddle below.

I can only imagine the excitement the first cattle guards brought to people in rural America. No longer did the trip to town mean opening and closing twenty-five gates. Instead, these magic metal fittings kept the cows in the right field and they could drive right on through. What an engineering breakthrough!

But now they are so commonplace, we complain if they're not perfect.

On a recent drive with our son, Tom, we each cleared our seats by a couple of inches as the pickup flew over a cattle guard just inside our white gate. "The worst cattle guard on the place," he grumbled. And I thought back on the eggs I'd broken at just that spot coming home from town.

Cattle guards serve as landmarks for the trip to our ranch. My favorite is at the top of the summit between our neighbor's place and ours. From that height you can see ridge line after ridge line reaching up and into the Pioneer mountain peaks. "Stop at the cattle guard," I suggest to friends coming from town. "Touch the space. This is the top of the world."

Recently, our sheep manager told us a story told him by a Forest Service employee. At a congressional hearing, the employee told committee members there were something like 15,000 cattle guards on Forest Service lands, to which a lawmaker replied, "Well, let's fire some of them and save some money."

"How can we talk together when people don't even know what a cattle guard is?" our manager asked despairingly. And I realized how different the language of the West can be and how important it is for us to become patient translators.

Rodeo Heroes

I HAVE ALWAYS LOVED RODEOS. When I lived in the East, I'd plan western trips around them. I'd sit in wooden stands, in dusty arenas, in the hot sun, and dream of throwing off my traditional job for the rodeo life. Although today I watch my husband and our cowboys rope and ride daily at our cattle ranch, my blood still races when I walk around a rodeo arena, smell the stock, and see the cowboys milling around until their time to ride.

And I was inspired again last summer at the Twin Falls County Fair. All night the rodeo announcer's comments over the loudspeaker on cowboys, cowtowns, and cowboying skills competed with other noises of the fair. I was wandering through exhibit buildings and barns, around the carnival and food stalls. I didn't listen too much.

Not until I found myself trapped in a line of cars waiting to get out to the highway did I pick up on the rodeo, and then only because I was suddenly struck by the urgency and excitement of the announcer's voice booming over the sound system. He was describing the barrel race—that tough riding event saved for the female gender.

"Next up," he began, "Charmayne Rodman, a real champion. This little lady is the only barrel racer to make over a million dollars. One million dollars," he repeated, clearly impressed. "Let's give Charmayne a real big Twin Falls welcome."

Then came the shocking words of unadorned admiration: "What a woman!" he burst out. "What a horse!" Or was it "What a horse! What a woman!"? Never mind. What stayed with me was the word "woman." Not "little lady" or "little girl" or any of the other distinctly cute phrases uttered by announcers and cowboys alike when they're uncomfortable. "What a woman!" he had said.

What a statement! I thought as I pulled onto the highway. The news of

Charmayne's 17.1 score, which put her in fourth place, faded into the night. Tough luck, Charmayne.

I stopped for gas and an errand, then headed my car for the interstate. As I did, I noticed ahead of me a pickup pulling a fancy horse trailer trimmed entirely in dazzling white lights. I pulled up behind it and swallowed hard as I read the scrolled lettering: "Charmayne Rodman nine times World Champion Barrel Racer."

I couldn't believe it. Charmayne right here on the same road! On the right panel I read "A Sundowner Trailer," then in quotes, "I love it," which I could only guess was Charmayne's assessment of the trailer, or rodeoing, or maybe just life in general. "I love it."

I edged ahead, hoping for a glimpse of Charmayne herself, but instead I saw a young, good-looking, rodeo-type guy driving, laughing, and chewing on a Polish sausage tucked in a fat roll. Next to him, hidden in the darkness of the front seat, Charmayne was probably telling stories.

It was not more than thirty minutes since she had ridden, and now she was on the road, eating greasy fair food, headed toward another dusty rodeo arena, another string of barrels, another chance at money, and another quick escape from the noise and crowds. Carried off in the dark in her top-of-the-line chariot, telling her story to the world in scrolled lettering, "I love it!"

Myth and Reality

OFTEN I BALANCE on the thin ledge between myth and reality, a position I understand better now after a trip to the Midwest.

I was invited to read my stories at the second Annual Illinois Cowboy Poetry Gathering, an idea that amused me because I don't think of Illinois as a cowboy state and I don't think of my stories as cowboy poetry. But I had read at the winter Cowboy Poetry Gathering in Elko, Nevada, and was spotted by the Illinois organizer, who extended the invitation immediately. I confess I was also intrigued by the idea of cowboy poetry in the chic Chicago suburbs of Winnetka.

When my plane ticket arrived, I went into a panic realizing that in Illinois, I would walk the fine line between myth and reality. I must look and behave like a cowboy poet, which meant getting all duded up because those "ole boys" and women do dress to recite their works. I'm talking red and purple boots, mother-of-pearl stud buttons and lots of fringe.

I took small comfort from the words of a ranch woman I had heard read her poems in Elko, remembering how she looked down at her pants tucked into her fancy blue boots and laughed. "I wouldn't be caught dead looking like this back on the ranch," she allowed. "But here, well, what the heck."

There it was: the myth and the reality.

But still I cringed at the idea of putting on jeans and boots in the murky midwestern summer. So I packed an old blue-jean skirt and a sleeveless denim shirt but stopped at the boots, wondering if I could bear to put them on in the 105-degree heat. At the last minute, I threw them in my bag.

At O'Hare Airport a young volunteer met me in jeans, a T-shirt, boots, and straw hat. This kid looked like a cowboy. I reached the hotel to see several hats, full mustaches, and boots on male figures wandering through the lobby. I already felt out-of-place in my shorts and sandals.

In my room I unpacked solemnly. I had nothing with fringe, no hat. I was an impostor. No one would ever believe I lived on a sheep and cattle ranch.

The first performer that evening was a pretty girl who sang about rodeo queens and hard-riding cowboys. They were swing tunes, she suggested, that should "get yer toes a-tappin'." But midway through her performance, she admitted to the audience that she and her husband had to leave their South Dakota ranch and move to Illinois for work. She sang a wistful song of this experience. I was startled to hear of this separation but not her longing. It was a story that appeared and reappeared in the words of other poets throughout the evening.

I soon understood that a number of these cowboy poets have lost their farms and ranches and now hold on to the life they loved through their words, through myth and memory. I also understood that I was one of the few there that night still ranching, one of the few who still lives with the beauty and wildness of the land, with the hard work and solitude of the life, even though others look the part better than I.

And suddenly I realized that my stories may be less sentimental and may be told without fringe, without mother-of-pearl buttons, but it is important that they be told—for all of us—for those we lost and for the few of us who remain.

Terrorism Tamed

THE CHILLING TERM "TERRORISM" has become a part of every American's vocabulary. But I was startled to find its hand upon my life in the person of my husband. He is, in fact, a terrorist. There is no kinder term for his behavior. His cause is lamb, and as a tireless advocate for this product he makes industry promotion men look plain lazy.

I first noticed his quirky campaign at restaurants. Dining out with him became embarrassing and I soon was left to wonder why any of our friends wanted to spend an evening with us.

We were seated at a table. He scanned the menu. No lamb. The waiter arrived. "I'll have the lamb chops, please," my husband perversely placed his order. The young man looked stricken. "We have no lamb," he explained, which was my husband's cue.

"I thought this was a quality restaurant. No lamb? I can't believe it," he announced to the waiter loud enough to be heard at the tables around us. "Tell the manager that we are disappointed and we will think twice before coming here again." The rest of us looked at the possibility of crawling under the table.

Scenario two. Lamb was on the menu. "Where is your lamb from?" my husband politely asked the waitress. Invariably she had to check with the chef, and woe to the news that the lamb was imported. "New Zealand!" my husband bellowed so that once again everyone in the restaurant could appreciate the event. "How could you? I thought this was a quality restaurant. Tell the manager . . ."

Occasionally he ordered the meat without asking the country of origin, and when the tiny imported chops appeared on his dinner plate, he began. "You call this lamb?" he roared, again for all to hear. "These little chops are mostly bone. This must be frozen lamb from New Zealand. It is a slap in the face to local producers. I could be eating Idaho mountain-fed lamb. And furthermore," he moved in for the kill, "New Zealand chops are just like chicken. You need sauce to give them any flavor at all. Tell your manager I thought this was a quality restaurant." And so on.

But this was only the beginning of my husband's campaign. His most terrifying performance took place at the supermarket, where lamb, the underdog so to speak, cried out, today still cries out, for consumer support. Here, in decoratively displayed rows of meat, the number-one enemy, chicken, brashly seizes the limelight. And I confess I shudder when I see this product spilling across large sections of the area in pursuit of public attention. Hogging, if you'll pardon the term, a huge share of space.

But not for long. We enter the store. I head for the produce section. My husband heads for the meat. When I catch up to him, he has tipped all the Styrofoam trays of chicken on end so the blood and water collect in a pool at the bottom of the dish. It is an appalling sight guaranteed to make any shopper think twice. But I'm not sure which is more alarming, the new chicken display or my husband chortling at his handiwork.

If I can get to the meat section in time, I can keep him from rearranging the display—easing the tiny 6-inch column saved for lamb into 20 inches of chops and shanks spilling recklessly over the pork on one side, the beef on the other. I only wait for the day I am called to bail him out of jail for meat-display tampering.

But this chicken-as-enemy thing is the most serious. Recently he brought me an article from a farm magazine and danced around the room as he jabbed at the headline: "Chicken and water." Then he read aloud from the text. "Under current federal regulations, poultry processors are allowed to add up to 8 percent water to chickens and 9 percent water to turkeys. Consumers purchase a total of 925.4 million dollars in water every year." Ah ha. He gloated, "What did I tell you?" as if I needed the lesson.

He excels at dinner parties. "It is a mystery," he has been heard to comment at buffet tables, "why people continue to eat chicken laced with tetracycline and full of salmonella. Guests smile, nod, and look anxiously at their plates of Chicken Bombay or Coq au Vin.

Once I served an elaborate chicken dish to dinner guests only to have my husband the terrorist announce as we were seated, "I'd like to apologize for this entree. It's probably loaded with salmonella. I can't understand why

Diane is serving it, when she could have grilled some lamb." There is no food for him but lamb.

But there is a follow-up tale to all of my husband's antics. It began with a nasty, nagging sense that we should be doing something more substantial than simply complaining. For example, perhaps we could respond to requests from friends and Sun Valley chefs who wanted our lamb in local restaurants.

My husband and I knew this would not be easy. Flat Top Sheep Company is no small ranch, and when we send lambs to market it is eight hundred at a time, often more. I shuddered at the idea of breaking apart our outfit for ten to twenty lambs a week that would need special treatment.

But after enough complaining, we were stuck. We approached several of the best local chefs and found them immediately enthusiastic. Yes, they'd love to serve "natural, mountain-fed, lamb," they told us. A meatpacker in Boise was also interested in our idea, as was a meat cutter in Buhl. The latter suggested he cut several carcasses into samples for prospective chefs. One shoulder he turned into steaks, the second into stew meat. On a second carcass he cut a third shoulder into a perfectly rolled roast, and the last became quality lamb burger. Of course there were trimmed racks, chops, and legs. Then, holding bundles of cryovacked meat nestled in display boxes I took a deep breath and walked into a restaurant kitchen.

Its owner picked up a piece of meat, studied it briefly, and before I could launch into my all-natural pitch, he began his list. "I'd like fifty steaks, twenty pounds of lamb burger, and all the shanks you can get me." I couldn't believe it.

The next morning there was a message on our answering machine from another chef who had sampled our meat. "Diane, your product is fantastic. I want all I can get." I saved his message for days. Next the local gourmet market agreed to carry our meat, and Sun Valley Lamb was officially launched.

Today the dilemma is this: The praise is inspiring. The work is exhausting. Weekly, all summer, we run between the packing plant, meat cutter, and clients with our precious cargo. These events require huge amounts of special attention and physical labor—lifting, loading, and hauling. It is a significant personal cost. And although we are selling the meat at premium prices, our work shaves off much of the profit.

Yet this effort has slowed my husband's campaign of terrorism, and I secretly hope that between his subtle sabotage and our small attempts to bring our meat to local markets, Idaho lamb might become the treasured item it should be. Who knows, we just might sway the minds and hearts of the great American public. Then we can retire, content that our bold convictions have become mainstream, or at least main course.

Hollyhocks

WHEN I RETURN to the ranch each spring, I walk the ground outside my bedroom window and along the back of the cabin, looking for the broad flat leaves that mean there will be hollyhocks this summer. I may find one plant or five or six. They come back randomly, in new places each year.

Someone planted them long ago and they still survive the deep snows of winter and wild grasses that threaten to crowd them out each summer. They bloom deep red, white, or pale pink, changing color coquettishly each year. They are the miracle of my summers.

For several years, I tried to expand the spotty crop with a packet of seeds along the fence but without success. I should have known. Although tall, tough grasses and cottonwood shoots grow in profusion, little else makes it through the stubborn soil. I have failed in all my attempts to add wildflowers, sunflowers, or even spruce trees to the mix despite hours of watering and weeding.

So I am amazed by the stamina of these hollyhocks, and I wait breathlessly through June and July until they reach full height and bloom in August. They have become a kind of metaphor for my life on this remote ranch. We are the survivors.

In the full rush of unrelenting summer activity, the business of ranching pushes us. There is round-the-clock cutting, raking and baling hay, combining barley. There are hot days spent moving the cattle through the hills and the sheep camps behind bands of lambs and ewes. There are sweaty hours of sorting the heifers and yearlings through the dusty corrals. Ranching demands hard work and long days that cannot be abandoned for vacations. We move fast, sleep little, and hang on.

This morning, when I saw the first blush of pink outside the cabin, I was reminded of this endurance. Almost as I blinked, two hollyhocks, like bookends on a single stalk, blossomed, the only color in the snaggle of brown brush beyond the fence. And in this moment, I understood suddenly why summer is my favorite season. Every day brings surprise. In my yard the flowers cycle new color and fragrance. Tulips, then iris, and when these fade the poppies and columbine appear, then daisies and Sweet William. There is no time to tire of one flower before another blooms in its place.

It is this way too with the tastes of summer. When spicy radishes are all picked, there are crisp carrots, then succulent lettuce and chard leaves, sweet corn and tomatoes, and finally raspberries that turn red on thick bushes.

Summer is the time of flowering. But none more inspiring than holly-hocks. They return without coaxing, the best of summer's abundance. And they appear when we most need it—when we grow tired of too much heat, too many exhausting days of hard ranch work—as if to remind us of the meaning of tenacity. What greater inspiration than these stalks of blooms, deep red, pale pink, come back again, come home.

Bull Meat

THE FIRST TIME I fully realized how far I was from town at my new husband's ranch was shortly after the hulking Black Angus bull fell between the rungs of a cattle guard. It was a harrowing night as we joined ranch hands using heavy machinery to extract the animal from his trap. But the trauma and injury proved too much for the huge bull. We could not save him.

This animal's subsequent conversion into hundreds of little white packages of ground beef turned into a nightmare. His tragedy became mine.

Although the meat was distributed to families throughout the ranch, I ended up with a disproportionate share, or so it seemed. I vowed to use the meat, which, I rationalized, would save hundreds of dollars in groceries and win the undying respect of my new husband and his family.

I started off with hamburgers. What better use of ground meat? But despite their succulent appearance, they were inedible—tough, dry, and tasteless. Undaunted, I tried spaghetti sauce, then chili, then Greek moussaka. But this beast had not an ounce of fat on him. No fat, no taste.

I continued to experiment but dinnertime became unbearable. Conversation at the table ceased, only to be replaced by intricate chewing rhythms and grunts. Our appetites shrank. The entire family began to lose weight. Only the dog prospered, swelling up on table scraps, or rather on portions considerably larger than scraps.

One afternoon while peering into the freezer cavity still bulging with bull meat, I realized in despair that there was no pizza a phone call away and no one to provide any gastronomic relief out here 24 winding miles from town. It was the bull and me.

As this thought settled, I turned frantic. It was a lazy summer afternoon but my shrieking and pleading reverberated through the quiet. I ordered all those little white packages gone, calling, I feared, hopelessly into the wind.

But twenty-four hours later, when I looked into the big white freezer, the meat was gone and a new sweet emptiness called back to me. Joyfully, I jumped in the car and drove the washboard road to town, only one thought in my mind: a juicy, tender steak, rich flavor exploding in my mouth with every bite. Maybe I'd even bring home a pizza.

Fences

MY HUSBAND AND I have an arrangement about who opens the gates when we drive around the ranch. Normal range practice dictates that the passenger, often a code word for "wife," jumps in and out, over and over, to open and close the gates. But instead, my husband tends to the gates while I drive the pickup through the opening.

At first I thought he did the work because the barbed wire and posts are so tightly assembled that loosening the loops at the top and bottom requires shoulder heaving and brute force. But one day it occurred to me: he loves opening the gates.

From the ground he can assess the fence and determine—as he always does—that it needs some work. Out comes a 3-foot strip of barbed wire from the back of the pickup and moments pass as he tugs and twists, pliers flashing until he's satisfied that the gate or fence line is vastly improved. These events are absolutely predictable on every drive.

At the ranch, we have our share of fences up and down hillsides, around meadows, across ridge lines. The ranch hands spend days each year mending or replacing them.

But recently I have come to understand the pride my husband, and many other ranchers, feel for the perfect, straight-as-an-arrow fence. On a drive through our winter range, my husband pulled up along a line of stakes with pink streamers set out at regular intervals. They marked the direction of a new fence we were building. He got out, and from between the posts, stared down the line, closing one eye first, then the other, and frowned. "It's not straight," he grumbled when he returned to the truck.

The next day I heard him tell our sheep manager, "Those guys just aren't doing it like we'd do it." And for the next few minutes they went on about fences they had built in the old days.

I thought this was a little tedious until I heard a friend tell of her family ranch in Montana and the fences built with such care by her grandfather. "Straight as a string," she said. And I knew my husband would enjoy fences lined out "straight as a string."

Fences have changed the West. Barbed wire strung across once-wild lands cut off Indians from their traditional hunting grounds, provoking panic and war in a last bid for freedom.

For years the history of the West continued to be one of barbed wire, but it usually was to contain livestock, not to keep people off the land. I still see signs that say "Close gates behind you."

But today this history of fences has taken a new turn. With "tax-avoidance ranches" and hobby farms come neatly painted white fences and "No Trespassing" signs—their message reinforced by padlocked gates, or worse, coded security systems.

And I cannot help but fear that the West is moving in a painful new direction. That with these new fences, this land and its people are closing up, folding inward more swiftly and surely than we ever would through any range war.

Chief Joseph Days

THIS YEAR MY FAMILY came together from all parts of the country to celebrate our parents' fiftieth wedding anniversary. We gathered in Joseph, Oregon, on our small ranch in the Wallowa Valley in July, during Chief Joseph Days, a weekend of rodeos, parades, and cowboy dances. The event was the highlight of our summers when we were young.

But soon after we arrived, we were reminded that others too were there to honor their elders and family memories. Chief Joseph Days is named for the famous Nez Perce Indian chief and is held here because this was the homeland of Joseph's band of Nez Perce. Each year on this weekend the tribe returns, coming home.

The Nez Perce lost this country soon after settlers began to arrive. In a bid for freedom, they defied an order to move to the Lapwai Reservation near Lewiston. Instead they began a heroic trek that took the small band of families through Idaho and Montana in an attempt to reach the Canadian border and safety.

For months they outwitted the U.S. military, who chased them across rivers and over mountain ridges. But in the end, cold, hunger, and death loss forced them to surrender. They were unaware that they were only 40 miles from the Canadian border and freedom. It was then that Chief Joseph spoke his haunting words, a part of which were: "Our chiefs are killed . . . the old men are all dead . . . it is cold and we have no blankets. The little children are freezing to death. . . . Hear me, my chiefs! I am tired. My heart is sick and sad. From where the sun now stands I will fight no more forever."

My father, a writer and historian, brought us to this valley over thirty-nine years ago when he was researching a book on the Nez Perce. Many of our first western friends were from the tribe. They stayed with us over Chief Joseph weekend before the town provided space for an encampment in a downtown park.

And so now my father, sister, husband, and I joined them for their annual friendship meal on Saturday noon by their teepees. In the shade of the picnic arbor we feasted on salmon and venison and listened to the elders speak in their slow, clear rhythms.

They thanked the community for letting them return, for their friendship, and, as one said, "for the opportunity for our elders to feel well for several days." They spoke of their pride as Nez Perce and told stories from their grandparents of life in this valley long ago.

As they spoke softly, my mind traced the landscape of our ranch in Idaho, its meadows and ridges. It is the place of my family's work, our dreams and our stories. It is home. But life on the land today is financially precarious. We struggle to stay. And I wonder, if we lost our home, could I return to our land each year with memories in my arms?

Under the arbor the Nez Perce prayed to slow drumbeats and the small chime of a single bell, the only sound in the afternoon stillness. A sadness swept over me for these people, and for all those denied the landscape where their hearts and stories live.

Fall

THIS IS THE SEASON *of golden grasses and burnt red leaves. Hillsides glow but darkness crowds the daylight morning and evening. It is the season of accounting, of adding the numbers, reviewing livestock costs and market prices, penciling in crop returns, while we try not to ask "what if" there had not been heavy spring rains, early fall frosts, plummeting market prices? Outside, flowers turn brown on tall stems in windowboxes. Yellow-orange days still warm us and hold us to this land. We treasure each moment but we know the chill air brings separation with it.*

Wolves

I REMEMBER CLEARLY the day my husband rushed into the kitchen and breathlessly told me he had seen a wolf. "He was a wonderful creature," he added, and for the rest of the day it seemed his mind was far away in the fields with the wild animal again.

Several months later, our cowboy told us he had heard a wolf one morning when he was gathering the team. He had the same wonder in his voice my husband had had weeks earlier.

These events are among my husband's favorite ranch stories. "I saw a wolf here about six years ago," he'll tell visitors, "and our man heard him several months later." For him it is part of the mystery of living on the land.

Recently my husband and I went to a Wolf Recovery program at a friend's house in the city. In the enclosed yard, two long-legged, gray-brown animals on leashes strained for attention. "Get down on their level," their owner advised. "Look them in the eyes and get to know them."

We did. Smelling their animalness, looking into their glassy blue eyes, I stroked their coarse fur and wondered what it must be like to see them in the wild. I thought about my husband's brief moment with one and I envied him the experience. We told a program leader about the wolf at our ranch. The excited young man ran to tell others. Each wolf sighting is an event.

Later that evening the hosts ran a film about these animals. My husband leaned forward in his chair as if he might join them in their mountain freedom. They howled on screen once, then again, and everyone in the room became silent, stunned by the chilling sound. My husband leaned even closer to the screen.

Then the image changed in front of us. A rancher was rounding up cattle and instantly I realized that he was the bad guy. Livestock, the narrator said, crowded out wolves. Now ranchers are resisting their reemergence, afraid the wild animals will kill their sheep and cattle.

I looked at my husband. He had drawn back and sat small in his chair. And I realized suddenly that we were the enemy for people looking for simple solutions and I felt isolated in this room of friends.

Sunday

ALTHOUGH THE LABOR DAY WEEKEND DRAWS the line between summer and fall, I am reluctant to let go of warm-weather memories and think back on a recent Sunday at our ranch—a day full of sights, sounds, and small lessons.

Early Sunday morning I sit on our cabin porch in the sunshine. The garden in front of me is crowded with all heights and shapes of white daisies that spill out onto the lawn. Across the yard is the old sheep wagon, its bed packed full of yellow and orange marigolds, pink cosmos, and red and white snapdragons. They seem to be brushing the sky from where I sit.

Beyond the fence, fields of tall grasses lead into sagebrush hills. There, Black Angus cattle graze in the quiet.

Suddenly the animals begin bawling. It seems too early in the season for calves to be weaned but I am too far away to see their size. My husband appears in the doorway.

"What is the racket?" I ask.

"Bulls," he laughs. "They are just bellerin' and bluffin' each other from a safe 100-foot distance. You know, sort of like a poker game at the men's club."

We eat breakfast at a picnic table in the shade of a spruce tree, then I read awhile, knowing that before the day is out, my husband will suggest a drive to check the grass, the crops, or the cattle. Perhaps all three. It's what we do on Sundays.

The offer comes in the afternoon. Our black and white Border collie Jock is first in the pickup. He's been waiting for this moment since sunup.

We head down the dirt road that skirts the canola field with its acres of bright yellow blossoms. My husband stops the truck. We get out and he picks several stems, then from the other side of the road and another field, he pulls off a stalk of wheat. He gestures toward the three sandhill cranes at the end of the field. I nod. He brings me the stalks and points to the large seed pods hanging below the canola blossoms.

It is our first year with this crop. Like many in ranching, we continue to look for products to sustain our operation. Then he breaks off a kernel of wheat and pinches it open. It is milky inside, not ready yet.

We drive cross-country through the field of black cows. "These ol' girls are the oldest cows on the ranch," my husband comments. "They've never lost a calf and we take good care of them, baby them along." Their female offspring are valuable and will continue the line.

We maneuver the pickup from one group of cows to the next. "They're just baling up that grass," my husband laughs, proud of his livestock. "I've never seen as much feed as this year, or as little as last year," he adds.

Ryegrass some 4 feet tall brushes by the pickup window. Last year's dried stalks are a third that size, and I remember a year ago driving over drought-parched ground and through burned grasses.

By now the sun is low in the sky, coloring the clouds sandy pink and throwing stark light across the expanse of hills and ridges. For the first time I notice a chill in the mountain air. Soon cold weather will force us to leave our remote ranch home for the winter and we will pull up this day in our minds, as we might pull out old photos from a drawer, settling into its images again and again until we return next spring.

Rethinking Priorities

TWENTY YEARS AGO, I decided to move to Idaho, or more specifically to Flat Top Sheep Company Ranch—24 dirt-road miles from town.

But before I left the East Coast, I spent two days in Bloomingdale's in a shopping frenzy, scooping up a set of silverware and china just a touch fancy, new wine and fluted champagne glasses, a European coffeemaker, among other items. Satisfied with these treasures, I headed to a favorite bookstore to collect a few classics, some poetry, and the latest novels. Then on to a large record shop and finally a gourmet food store for exotic spices and condiments.

This spending spree was inspired by the nagging fear that once I made my historic move, I would somehow find myself deprived in my ranch isolation. Or more to the point, I was the tiniest bit afraid that my new life would be filled with terrifying challenges and that I might need these familiar treasures for courage and solace.

For days after I arrived at Flat Top, a fleet of boxes followed me, hauled home by ranch hands collecting the mail. I was a bit embarrassed. But never sorry. For I know that without these reminders of my independent days, those first awkard and lonely years in cowboy country would have shattered any self-confidence I brought with me.

But now I look back on this seemingly strange performance and decide it was not really so unusual. I was simply responding to this move west as many women have before me. For example, my mother-in-law often tells of Florence, her mother, hauling trunks of silver and china with her from Kansas to Idaho in the early 1900s when she moved here with her husband.

And certainly journals of early pioneers on the California and Oregon trails poignantly recount stories of the family treasures and household wares that travelers were forced to leave along the trail in order to lighten their loads for the arduous trip. For them it was often a choice of saving the silver tea service or the weary horses hauling a dying child inside a covered wagon.

I wonder. What did we expect of this place? What deprivation, what empty space, so frightened us that we needed to hold on to our past to embrace the future?

And now, eighteen years later, I look around me at my life at Flat Top and realize that most of these treasures are scratched or chipped or have been put away almost unused. I really don't drink champagne that much after all. Oh, perhaps when we have an exceptional hay crop or lamb prices sneak mischievously high.

Although there was a time when these things mattered, I am now like the families on the Oregon Trail who quickly threw the trappings from another life off the wagon to save a sick child. For we have our own desperate moments living on this remote ranch, some brought about by startling economic inconsistencies, others by tragic natural disasters.

And at these times I, like those early pioneers, can reset priorities with shocking ease. Because for me what matters now is this life lived on the land. It is what I fight for each day. In the shifting priorities, those once-valuable china pieces are now of so little consequence.

Chokecherry Jelly

MARY, MY MOTHER-IN-LAW, drives her gray car up to the gate of the house. Dogs and canes spill out when she opens the front door to pull herself from the driver's seat. What could she want now? I wonder.

Mary and her friend Gertrude are making chokecherry jelly, and already Mary has driven twice from her rambling green house behind the ranch cook shack to our small cabin on the creek in pursuit of something to keep the chokecherry project alive.

"Any more jars?" she asks. She already has every jelly jar I own. I hand her a box of large wide-mouth pints not really suitable for jelly, but she leaves delighted.

I smile at the thought of Mary and Gertrude, two eighty-four-year-old, silver-haired women leaning over a steaming kettle of boiling berries and sugar-water thickening into sweet red jelly. But the real wonder of the event is Mary, my mother-in-law, making chokecherry jelly for the first time in her life.

Even though she has spent many summers at this remote place surrounded by bushes heavy with this fruit, she is only now discovering its mysteries at the urging of her friend. It was Gertrude who arrived earlier in the day with buckets of berries and Gertrude who now leads Mary through the delicious steps from fruit to jelly.

Gertrude spent her childhood years roaming this country and learning the locations of all the best bushes. Then she left the ranch to follow her dreams. Meanwhile, Mary led a different life.

The daughter of a U.S. senator, Mary was also the wife of another. Early in life, she developed a keen sense of politics and rose to become assistant chair of the national Republican Party and ultimately director of the U.S. Mint under Presidents Nixon and Ford. Pictures in her home show

Mary with four different U.S. presidents. Sometimes it is hard to find time to make chokecherry jelly, but it's never too late.

Now the two silver-haired women laugh and pour the sweet, red liquid into waiting jars. They finish late in the afternoon in time for Mary's favorite TV show. Reluctantly Gertrude joins her to watch reporters debate political events, but she can't hide a slight scowl as she wonders what Mary sees in all the fuss.

Relaxed at last after their day of work, the two women sip from plastic green glasses filled with vodka and settling ice cubes. Occasionally one or the other will look up from the screen to sniff the lingering smell of chokecherries now locked tightly in assorted jars on the kitchen counter, and each, in turn, will smile.

The Road

THERE ARE TWO ROADS into our ranch. One heads north from the small town of Carey with its new 6 miles of once fancy-paved, and now deeply potholed, surface before it turns to dirt. It runs absolutely straight through wide-open landscape almost the entire distance from town to the ranch. It's the easy way home.

The second road starts in Bellevue and follows an arduous 24-mile route east that climbs and plunges, twists and turns, through moments of unsettling beauty. It is this road that connects the ranch to the bustling business community and the county seat. In the late 1800s, it was used by miners to haul silver and lead from the Muldoon mines behind our ranch into town.

Later, the Laidlaws drove this route in a horse and buggy. It was a two-day trip for them along a road with fifty-two gates to open and close round-trip. Today the gates are gone but some of the perils remain.

The road is completely unreliable. In winter it is closed. In early spring, snowmelt makes it too muddy to drive. In summer it is a dusty washboard and in the fall it turns to mud again if the rains start early. But driving it, when it's open, is worth the risk.

The road begins at Highway 75. Almost immediately it is swallowed up by the narrow Muldoon Canyon. This stretch cuts through the EE-DA-HO ranch—with its perfect white fences and designer house perched on the edge of a man-made lake. All this is at the base of an avalanche slide area. But then the whole narrow valley is avalanche country.

The last owners, frustrated with cars that raced along the road through their ranch (probably people like me), persuaded the county to build a second road outside their fence line. When it was completed, it was a steeply pitched, terrifying detour that hung from the hillside at what seemed to be a 75-degree angle. It was never used much and now is partially covered in weeds as drivers race across the easier, and faster, old road through the ranch. The new absentee owners don't seem to mind, or maybe they just don't know.

The landscape begins to open up as the road climbs in wide sweeping arcs around sagebrush hills to a summit. There, at the cattle guard that divides the E-DA-HO from our ranch, this breathtaking expanse stretches across ridge lines for miles into the Pioneer Mountains in the distance.

The road then descends through aspen groves and wildflowers into Cold Springs Canyon, where cattle graze in the summer and natural springs green the hillsides long after other areas have turned brown. Several miles farther is the small log cabin that sits over a spring where early travelers stopped for water on the way to and from town.

The road moves through shady aspen groves and between beaver ponds before it turns to the right at the sheep corrals. There it follows the Little Wood River passing some of the best chokecherry bushes on the ranch. It climbs again steeply until it opens out onto our hay and grain fields. There it merges with the road from Carey. Around the corner, the landmark rock with its imposing profile of a man's head fills the landscape, and just beyond is the whimsical county highway sign that warns drivers of "loose cattle."

In this last stretch, sweeping meadows come alive with antelope and deer that graze side by side with the livestock. The bottomland belongs to a neighbor until you get close to our white gate and can see the seventy-year-old Laidlaw fence marking off the land to the south.

Today, I drive from Bellevue to the ranch in forty-five minutes. There are no gates to open and close but it is still isolated. Often I wonder what Mrs. Laidlaw busied her mind with as she traveled this road to town and back much more slowly than I. And as familiar as I am with this route, I envy her intimacy with this landscape and wish I could have joined her on her journey just once.

Pickup Talk

THERE IS ONLY ONE really indispensable tool of the trade on a ranch—aside from a horse and saddle, of course—and that's the pickup. As a location for the men, it easily outdistances anything else for the "where most often found" category. But ownership carries with it strict standards of appearance that allow ranchers to easily spot a working outfit from a city slicker's rig.

First, a good ranch pickup should be filthy. A dusty film must disguise the vehicle's true color for most of the summer and slashes of mud and lumps of earth should cling to its body after a good rain. Of course, some cowboys will wash the truck before a Saturday night trip to town or taking the family to church on Sunday, but most of the time it is best that the pickup bear the scars of weather. It is a sort of mantle of authenticity.

If you can determine the color of the vehicle under the dust and mud, you will know how old it is. These days car dealers seem to stock one color a year. So if the pickup is red, it's probably a '91. If it's white, it's a '92. But the dirt is seasoning of its own.

The rig has standard features. It has a windshield with a crack trailing like a highway map across its surface or, at a minimum, it is pockmarked from flying rocks. There will be a hitch for pulling a horse trailer either under the tailgate or at the center of its open box.

And the pickup is outfitted with standard equipment. The owner's dog, for starters. This devoted companion will be hanging out the back if the truck's in motion, or sleeping in the corner by the tailgate when it's parked. This creature may be the only one in the world who loves the pickup better, and spends more time in it, than its owner.

As the dog snoozes in the sun, his paws will be wrapped around an old stay thrown in the back by the boss last May when the man thought he'd drive the ridge line to fix fence. In November, both dog and stay still languish in the back.

Around the dog and post is a confusion of treasures that includes strands of barbed wire to mend a gate, a jack to change flats, an old shovel for mud emergencies, and often a couple of blocks of salt to drop off for the cattle if the owner ends up driving through the back hills.

The inside of the pickup is also coated with dust. A toolbox rattles behind the front seat. Mementos cover the dash, matches, scraps of papers with telephone numbers, gloves with cow counts written in ballpoint pen on the back. A small calendar with line drawings and corny ranch jokes is pasted next to the radio knobs. Sunglasses and binoculars are in the pocket next to the driver's seat, and a couple of seed caps hang on the gearshift for windy days when a cowboy hat won't stay put. In many vehicles there is the ever-ready rifle in the rack on the back window. In newer pickups it is concealed overhead for easier access.

If I served him dinner in the pickup, I might never see my husband. It is the man's favorite location. His red rig has been run hard and has hauled plenty in its 152,000 miles. But still he'd rather be roaming the countryside in his truck than most anything else.

I can understand. Driving the roads of the West brings with it a sense of freedom and adventure that can take you farther and farther from the everyday into that backcountry you've only stared at from distant highways. But you must have a pickup to really explore ranch life.

Picture this: You've got your outfit (the cowboy term for "pickup") with dog and dust. You're ready to head over to the ranch for a real adventure. This immediately brings up the serious issue of directions. My advice is to follow the ranch owner the first time, if you want to get there. For some reason most of them are unable to explain how to drive roads they use regularly.

An example: You've followed the directions. You've crossed the bridge and now you are supposed to turn right after you pass the lower pasture. You look around. Is this grassy field to the right the lower pasture, or is it the field just beyond the fence line ahead? Could the land to the left of the road be the lower pasture? You edge past five trails that shoot off to the right, stopping at each to size it up. You move deeper and deeper into strange country, beginning to fret over your tires and the rocks kicking up around your new rig.

When you make the trip with someone who knows the place, you fly by the turnoffs and the road of choice seems obvious. Furthermore, you'll learn pickup etiquette firsthand and fast.

So now, instead, you're in the truck with the ranch owner. Get your role straight. If you're the passenger by the door, you will open and close the gates. This means wrestling taut barbed-wire loops off gnarled fence posts and then dragging hanging posts and wire across dusty ground to clear the way for the pickup. This is tough work. Try to sit in the middle and let someone else have the window seat.

More pickup protocol: Do not wave at the driver of a passing truck. Instead use the cowboy greeting. Just raise and lower the forefinger on the hand holding the top of the steering wheel. Your neighbor will do the same.

I confess that when I first saw this lazy finger motion, I thought it looked more disdainful than friendly, but now that I've got the hang of it from hand placement to finger motion, I am thrilled when another driver fingers back.

There is the more lengthy greeting that takes place at a backroad intersection when two pickups pass each other. Instead of driving by, they stop at the corner, one rig pointed east, the other nose west (or north and south, if you will) so the drivers can talk across the open windows.

I've passed neighbors in this holding pattern on my way to town and found them still there a half hour later when I return. These are the same neighbors who usually have little to say on the phone, in town, at church, or to their wives, but there seems to be something satisfying and safe about the confines of the pickup.

It is this, I think, that keeps my husband and so many ranchers and farmers pickup-bound. This workhorse of a companion, this dusty, muddy vehicle, may be the only thing they can count on in ranching today. And so it becomes for them a kind of safe haven in an otherwise incomprehensible world.

Running

RUNNING. I STRETCH one leg in front of another, reaching out farther and farther with each step. This exaggerated stride is a game, a momentary distraction to get me through my 3-mile run. I glance around me at the vast open space on both sides of this isolated ranch road and take in the same view I took in a mile ago, and realize that not a lot changes on a half-hour run when there is this much open country.

Before moving to Idaho I easily jogged down urban streets and parks, distracted by the changing scenery of gardens, houses, and shop windows. I was fully entertained. The time flew by.

But when I moved to this ranch, running became an endless experience. Distant mountains and buttes that framed the landscape looked remarkably similar one mile to the next. Yet I was determined to exercise. And no strolling through the wildflowers. If I was going to take the time, it had better be the serious heart-pumping stuff.

Over the years I've tried to persuade family members to join me, thinking company will make it easier. They all protest, hot and sweaty from cutting hay, baling it, fixing fence, or rounding up cattle. "We've worked too hard," they argue. "Work is not the issue," I explain. "The issue is moving your body." I point to the pickups that dart from the barn to the cook shack to the corrals and back again all day. "No one around here even walks," I add. "We're hauling things," comes the reply.

I give up, knowing I lost the battle before I even started. First of all there's no shade on these open roads so any exercise has to happen well before the heat of the day, which is also the busiest time at the ranch, for the same reason. Then there is this view issue.

So I head down the dirt road alone. And this is what I've come to appreciate.

First there is a cattle guard, so I can rest right away as I stop running to tiptoe across it. Then about five minutes into the trip are two cottonwood trees, which throw small patches of shade across my path. I spend a lot of time sizing up the distance and savoring the fleeting relief from the sun when I reach them.

I squint ahead looking for the small hump in the road where it crosses the irrigation ditch. This is followed immediately by another cattle guard with another chance to stop and catch my breath—after all, I am at 6,000 feet elevation.

Then the crops begin. A wheat field continues interminably until, just as I decide we've dug up the whole place for wheat, the color changes from yellow to green and the alfalfa begins.

Recently there was a windshield wiper on the road, which at first I thought was a snake. Once I realized what it was, I began to look for it each day. Then someone picked it up.

Last month the bulls were put in the first field and I spent quite a while building trust with the hulking black bodies blocking the road. "Hi, guys," I'd call out in my most soothing tones, slowing my pace so I wouldn't frighten them. "Don't let me bother you, just passing through. No threat here." It worked.

Now I've come to love this run where the scenery moves slowly. Where a lot and nothing happen all at once. And I'll continue to push myself forward looking for the small things in this vast space, because that's about all there is when the landscape passes one acre at a time.

Shearing

THIS WEEK WE ARE SHEARING our ewes. The light blue camp wagons pulled into the ranch on Sunday, the paint peeling off the wooden frames. The two wagons, with eight stations for eight men to work the ewes, were hooked together and backed up to the sheep corrals.

In the early days of the ranch, when we wintered the animals in Idaho, we sheared in the spring so the sheep would have full coats the next winter. But now we shear in the fall just before the ewes are sent to California to have their lambs in warm climates.

For five days the crew handles as many as 1,000 sheep a day. The air hums outside the camp from a small generator that provides the power for the razors and for the bare bulbs that dimly light the dark interior. Inside, the men straddling the animals lean over, actually ride, thick leather straps on pulleys that go up and down with their movements. The straps take the pressure off their backs as they wrestle the 170-pound sheep into position, then deftly move clippers across the wooly bodies. The shears are at the end of long rods that hang from the ceiling and bend like a dentist's drill to maneuver more easily.

The animals move up a ramp and along the inside wall of the camp wagon. When the men lift a panel door along the alley, the next ewe leaps from the chute into the arms of the shearer. After they are shorn, they are sent down a wooden ramp to the small pen outside. There they are branded—stamped—with green paint that stencils the symbol we describe as dot-bar-dot, like a large division sign, on their backs. It is our sheep brand that traces its beginnings to the early days of the ranch. Then, bounding out of the pen, the animals head off to drink from the creek behind our cabin under the yellow spread of cottonwood trees.

Behind the wagons, Sherry gathers the fleeces as they are pushed through the panel doors by the shearers. She ties them with cord and drops them by the packing machine. There Randy, the wool tromper, stuffs the bundles into a long, narrow burlap bag. A large mechanized plunger pushes the wool to the bottom of the sack. When it is tightly packed—with close to 300 pounds of wool—it is rolled out next to the other sacks ready for market.

"Before this machine," my husband tells me, "the sacks were hung vertically and a man stood inside stamping the wool down as it was dumped in overhead. That's how he got the name 'tromper'."

"You sure wouldn't want to be claustrophobic," adds our sheep manager, remembering the days when he was the kid in the sack.

The head of the shearing operation, Ed, has been leading a nomadic life for over thirty years shearing throughout Idaho, Nevada, and Oregon. "Used to be a time," Ed remembers, "when I'd be on the road eleven months a year, but there just aren't that many operations left and we're running out of shearers." He adds, "It takes time to train young guys. I've had four men ask to learn this year. I've taken on one but they're all slow at first and I can't keep up with the bigger outfits. Those shearing crews hire on twenty to thirty Australians and New Zealanders to take up the slack."

Ed looks old at forty-eight. Although his huge frame and muscled arms appear strong, his lined and sunburned face looks weary. Twenty-seven years is a long time to wrestle these large animals day after day.

That afternoon, I hear my husband as he negotiates with wool buyers on the phone for the fat sacks by the corral filled with the medium coarse wool characteristic of sheep from this region. It will be used for sweaters and blankets. I remember twelve years ago, we got 90 cents a pound for the fleeces. Several years later the price went to $1.16. Today wool is selling for 43 cents a pound. We cannot survive at these prices.

As I listen to my husband I realize, again, that the sheep industry is in jeopardy and I can't help but wonder how many more times we will see Ed's paint-chipped blue camp set up against our corrals on warm fall days like these.

Pahrump

IN 1984, WE BEGAN WINTERING our sheep and cattle in states with milder climates than that at our Idaho ranch headquarters. In pursuit of perfect pastures, we have crisscrossed Nevada and I have come to love this rugged, isolated state.

But in the beginning, I was not enthusiastic about its miles of primitive landscapes. I remember my horror when my husband first announced we were going to Pahrump. It was, he informed me, a place with excellent winter feed for the sheep. He had it on good authority from a rancher friend, who had heard about it from another rancher friend, who had heard about it from a Pahrump rancher friend. The alfalfa was second to none.

I had been whining for a vacation—but Pahrump? "Where is Pahrump?" I hissed.

"You'll love it," my husband kidded me. "It's in southern Nevada and it's warm and deserted."

My friends thought it was absurdly funny that I would end up in someplace called "Pahrump" for a vacation. I grudgingly helped packed the car.

In 1984, Pahrump was warm and it was deserted. But pink streamers fluttered on wooden posts across the landscape of open desert that overwhelmed this lonely spot on the road. Someone had already sized up the area. It was, after all, only 50 miles northwest of Las Vegas even though it clung to the edge of Death Valley.

Its few roads were mostly dirt. They stretched several blocks, then stopped abruptly at the edge of struggling alfalfa fields. From there, sand and desert brush extended flat for miles to the edge of mineralized red and gray mountains in the distance. There was a notable absence of the color green.

Pahrump had two motels. The first was trimmed in twenty-four-hour neon with a small, dark casino at its entrance. The second, The Carlotta, competed for the adult population with its queen-for-a-day, over-shagged, over-ruffled, powder-blue decor.

The town's culinary offerings included the smoke-filled café in the casino and the Cotton Pickin' Bar down the road that warmed up prepackaged tacos and enchiladas in its corner microwave. The Terrible Herbst Gas Station became an appealing dining alternative with its cellophane-wrapped sandwiches, canned goods, chips, and ice cream.

We were impressed to hear the town had an airstrip until we discovered it belonged to the Chicken Ranch, allegedly "The Best Little Whorehouse in Texas," now relocated in Pahrump. Of course we had to see this famous site and found it 7 miles outside of town, a sun-bleached trailer dumped in a sandy cactus patch. A double chain-link fence circled it and the parking area in front was deserted except for the frame of a dismantled car. At the airstrip in the distance, a ragged orange windsock hung limply from a rusted pole.

After several days touring the area with local farmers, we realized the spare alfalfa fields were not enough pasture for our sheep, so we moved on. It was four years later before we returned, and we did so then only after checking our band of sheep wintering in the lonely Armagosa Valley, 90 miles to the north.

As we approached Pahrump, I reached for the road map, thinking we had made a wrong turn. A golf course, a brilliant, almost hallucinatory shade of green, led the way into town. Trailer parks sprawled along the main road. Billboards crowded one another promising new condominiums. The Casino and The Carlotta motels were joined by several new ones all boasting "No Vacancy" in bright neon.

We pulled off the road into a new shopping mall with a supermarket, discount drugstore, pizza place, and video shop and stared around us until, confused and humbled, we were forced to acknowledge the obvious. There was no place for us in Pahrump anymore.

Rainbows

YESTERDAY WHEN I DROVE into the ranch there were three rainbows, actually four. One had a double arch. One fully spanned the sky, the others disappeared halfway up into fat gray clouds. Each time I stopped the car and peered out into the light rain to take a picture, it seemed the color faded as if the rainbows wanted to be only a memory, a dream.

It was typical of many stormy fall days at the ranch when dark clouds hang down almost touching the earth, then suddenly rise to release the sun—for just a moment. The most tranquil landscapes become deeply moody. The air is chilled. On the mountains around me I see a faint dusting of snow, "termination dust" they call it in Alaska, that first skiff of white in the high country that signals the end of summer.

And as surely as the leaves begin to turn brilliant orange after the first frost and flower stems turn brown in the hanging pots on the porch, the hunters arrive at our remote ranch in all manner and breed of four-wheel-drive vehicles.

The sky is just barely streaked with morning light when the knock comes at the door and familiar faces peer in the kitchen window. "Okay if we look for some birds in your hills?" one of the men asks. They are almost always men. There's coffee on and my husband and friends talk politics and weather for a while, then the hunters are on their way.

There are the first-timers, those unfamiliar cars that disappear down the road outside the ranch cabin unaware that it ends at our corrals. Minutes later they return, slipping past our house as if they hope we won't notice their wanderings out here with no other traffic.

Midmorning, my mother-in-law calls from her house just behind the white cook shack. "Twice this morning cars have pulled up to the house, then had to back out," she reports. "They were hunters thinking this was the road up Friedman Creek, no doubt." She took it well for an eighty-six-year-old woman by herself.

The worst part of hunting season is the arrival of a plaintive soul at the door late at night. He will bang until we get up and then ask if we'd come quickly to pull his truck out of a ditch.

My husband, a lifelong westerner, will respond far more generously than I, disappearing into the darkness to help the stranded stranger. I just pull the sheets over my head so I can sleep again.

On these gray days, those of us still at the ranch check in with one another from time to time feeling better that someone is nearby. Yet we savor the hours alone.

I remember when I first moved here. In early September, families of ranch hands moved to town when school started. Sometimes I was alone and, new to this quiet, I was frightened. But these days most of the kids have graduated and the ranch hands stay on longer into the year, getting ready to move the animals for the winter and close up this summer headquarters.

And the flurry of activity makes us all feel safe under the metal-gray sky. As if we are connected together by the land, by newly weaned calves bawling through the night, by bands of sheep down from the hills, by hunters in the backcountry, by frosted yellow leaves slick underfoot.

Or as if we are joined by rainbows across newly harvested fields, one, two, three—no, four—spans of color leading us through another season.

Trailing the Sheep

FALL AT OUR REMOTE IDAHO RANCH is a time for rounding up the animals, doctoring and tagging them, and shipping them to warm California climates. There, over the winter, they graze on leased pastures and have their young. For us the process begins when we bring in the cows from the hills and move the bands of sheep from the mountains north of the resort towns of Sun Valley and Ketchum to our ranch.

But in recent years, moving the sheep has become increasingly difficult as the exploding population of the Wood River Valley spills out onto formerly undeveloped lands in the Pioneer Mountain foothills. Newcomers to the area don't know that the history of this valley is the history of the sheep industry in the United States. They don't know that, at one time, the railroad—now long gone—hauled hundreds of thousands of lambs from the pens in Ketchum to markets in Ogden, Utah, each summer. And they don't know that most of the country now covered with houses or condominiums was once miles of open sheep pasture.

Nor do they understand that the bike path that cuts through the valley is also a sheep easement—the trail over which these animals traveled north in the spring and south in the fall for over a hundred years. And that this land was opened for biking and rollerblading only after sheep producers donated part of it to the county to carve out the recreational path.

Now this trail has become the source of controversy as the sheep make their seasonal move, angering its users who resent the days their bike path is soiled.

So my husband and I worried over the growing conflict until one evening, we came up with a plan. We would hold a "Running of the Sheep" and would ask the community to join us for the annual animal migration through the valley.

On a chill fall morning, we met at 6 A.M. at a local café, and over steaming cups of coffee my husband explained the history of the sheep industry in Idaho. He talked about our own operation, how we care for our animals, how we move them seasonally, how they feed only on natural grasses.

Then, just before the first light of day, with a group of thirty people, we headed out of town to join the herder with his band, to move the hundreds of white wooly animals south along Highway 75. With all of us there, we easily kept the sheep off the bike path, off the road, and running freely through the tall grasses.

In the morning, we moved the animals about 8 miles. In the afternoon we went another 6 through the populated area of Main Street Bellevue before turning east onto the dirt road to our ranch. After school, children joined in to herd the animals through the busy town between cars, signs, and wide-eyed pedestrians.

And when it was over, everyone collapsed, tired and dusty but understanding a little better about the place they call home. Understanding a little better the land and its mysteries, and most of all understanding a little better how the old ways can exist with the new.

Early Storm

"No chaps, no slicker, its pourin' down rain. I swear I'll never punch cattle again, com'a ti yi yippee yippee yea yippee yea."

My husband didn't sing often, but now he needed to take his mind off the dampness and cold that were making us all miserable. The late-fall snow caught us by surprise but the three huge livestock trucks had survived the slippery drive into our ranch, and cowboys and family were ready at the corrals to load them with cows.

The early-morning sky hung low and dark around us, hiding the mountains and buttes that usually defined this vast space. Fences, out-buildings, and familiar landmarks disappeared in the gray landscape. A quiet settled over the land.

It had started as snow earlier in the day and we had scrambled to find long underwear, gloves, and wool caps buried deep in drawers under summer clothes before heading out to the corrals. But as the morning wore on, the fat white flakes turned to rain, melting the hard ground into deep mud that shot up at us under animal hooves. All our clothing hung wet and heavy.

I noticed my husband, who always wore gloves, had none on. A gash on his hand was bleeding freely, cut on the gate he opened and closed as we counted the cattle onto the trucks. "Where are your gloves?" I called to him.

"Too wet," he called back. Two cowboys rode the end of the alley, yellow slickers in the mist.

The truckers, each dressed in coveralls, tall rubber boots, and seed company caps, tried to make light of the weather as they worked. They talked about their families, their own farming operations that they managed when they were not on the road, and, of course, the weather. "I'm not getting stuck on Donner. No way," one of the men called out for us all to hear.

We laughed. Another called out to my husband, "The snow will bring the elk to eat your hay." My husband shrugged.

"I had to turn off the water on my hay July 23 this year," the driver continued. "Instead of getting three cuttings, I only got a cutting and a third. This drought may force me out."

My husband shook his head and said, "In the old days we used to put up thirty to forty thousand bales of hay here. But that was when we wintered here, before this," his voice trailed off, as he nodded at the trucks and the cattle on their way to California pastures.

The animals loaded easily, pushing one another through the chute and onto the truck to get out of the wet and cold. The awkward, rumbling vehicles were another matter. They slid along the road and made wide swings in fields to turn around, slashing through whiteness and leaving behind clots of ruptured black earth.

Then one became stuck in the field. Someone went for the tractor. We waited. There were chains and men scrambling to hitch this, attach that. Slowly we pulled the helpless vehicle out of the grasping mud to the rocky ground at the end of the chute. Once it was loaded with animals, we held our breath as the driver eased away from the ramp.

"Go, Fred. Pull, pull!" someone yelled.

"Pull, you sonofabitch!" someone else joined in. Then came the cheers and whistles and Fred was on the road and on his way.

As I blew on red fingertips and waited for the next truck to pull up to the ramp, I remembered that I had planned to go to town that afternoon to hear Gretel Ehrlich read her ranch stories at the library. I checked my watch. I would miss her because of the storm, because of the cattle. I was disappointed for a moment, but after the second chorus of "Ti yi yippee, yippee yea," I realized I was caught in my own story on this gray fall day.

Rivers

I STARED AT THE SIGN along the road. It read "Save Our Rivers." Did people really understand what that meant? I wondered. Water is the issue that has manipulated the hearts and lives of so many of us in this arid landscape of southern Idaho. After too many years of drought, we look hard at what we have and what we have to lose.

We see irresponsible development drain the underground aquifer of the Snake River so low that neighbors dig their wells deeper and deeper to reach water for their homes, crops, and livestock. I hear stories that the lower end of the Big Lost River outside of Arco is dry, the life sucked out of the river by new upstream farming enterprises. Old-time family ranchers at the lower end of the valley are without water. My mind wanders back to Kansas and my husband's cousin, Blythe.

We visited her eight years ago when she was in her early nineties and still living at home. Blythe was our animated tour guide of three western Kansas counties, pointing out old pioneer sites and abandoned homes. But it was "Beaver Beach" I most remember, a long stretch of river that was the favorite swimming hole for Blythe and her friends when she was a young girl around the turn of the century.

As she told us stories of picnics and parties, we stared into a dry streambed with dead trees along the bank, brown and skeletal. Almost ninety years ago the river ran freely along Beaver Beach, fed by the sprawling Oglala Aquifer, a giant underground ocean of fresh water that sustained life from northern Texas to Nebraska. But as more settlers moved in and more irrigation wells pulled from the seemingly unending supply of water, its level was lowered and rivers began to dry up.

Several days ago I watched breathtaking scenes from the movie *A River Runs Through It,* the story of writer Norman Maclean growing up in

Montana. But the river he fished as a boy is so polluted they had to film his story elsewhere. And I thought of Beaver Beach in western Kansas.

Will we have the courage in the West to avoid the fate of communities who thought their water would last forever? Norman Maclean understandably was possessed by his river, ending his book with the chilling words "I am haunted by waters." Now we in Idaho might face our own ghosts if we allow our rivers to be sucked dry in careless contempt of tomorrow.

Farm Bill

I LOOKED AT the pale green paper flyer, an invitation to the "Forum on Farm Policy," a regional public meeting to discuss the next farm bill. It was time to revise national farm policy. It happens every five years.

In a sense I see my life in Idaho in five-year increments punctuated by congressional action on this issue. By the time the next farm bill is approved, I will have been here fifteen years and there will have been three bills. I think back on my life at Flat Top Sheep Company and my family's enduring struggle to survive on the land. I remember the years I worked for a farm organization in the late 1980s during the worst of the farm depression.

At that time, farmers were losing their operations and homes daily. There was confusion and anger in rural Idaho. In many cases small farms were absorbed into larger ones, dramatically reducing the number of people who lived on the land. Since then, much of that farmland has been incorporated into rapidly developing cities.

In an effort to understand what was happening, some farmers invited the then Texas commissioner of agriculture to Idaho. Jim Hightower, a small, fiery defender of family farms, told us to diversify. Seven acres of blueberries, he told a breakfast meeting of businessmen in Twin Falls, brought in enough cash for a farm family to subsidize its cattle operation. He also talked "value-added," thumping the podium with the zeal of an evangelical minister. "Don't just raise the crop. Do something with it, cuz if you don't, someone else will and they'll get all the money."

Finally he told us "get involved in this farm bill. You can plant, water, and harvest all you want, but if you're not paying attention to the politics, you'll lose the farm."

So we worked on the new farm bill and went back to Washington to testify. We tried to give the farm crisis a human voice. But in the 1988 presidential elections, there was little mention of farmers in any party platforms and few national candidates came to our towns.

Now after seven years of gut-wrenching drought we are called to action again by words on a green flyer. We will talk about sustainability of the land, fresh foods, and unpolluted waters. And we will talk about a fair price for commodities.

Yet we know even as we speak that in 1980, farmers got 37 cents of every food dollar and today we get only 26 cents. We know that the policies are wrong. We are told to get big or get out. We are advised by corporate buyers to use pesticides and herbicides so we can produce more, but we are flooding the market as prices spiral downward for those same corporations to buy our commodities at fire-sale prices. It is doublespeak spinning us around.

Yet we will testify and raise questions again about these policies, and once again we will suggest ways to survive, talk again about what might be possible for us in Idaho. We will talk about hope—about a better season, a better year . . . next year.

Town for Sale

WHENEVER THINGS GET TOO MUCH for me, I think about Grasmere, 32 miles from the Nevada line on Idaho Highway 51. This spot on the road sits bleakly in sagebrush and desert grasses, lonely, with mountains small and far against the distant horizon. A huge sign swings at the edge of the empty landscape. It reads "Town for Sale."

Intrigued, we turn off the highway and ease past a collection of battered cars and trucks, past a trailer house, and pull up next to the café. The round gas sign is gone, leaving only a rusted ring circling blue sky. The road-front display is Grasmere, the only sign of life for miles.

Inside the dimly lit room, the bartender and his one patron, sipping from an apple juice carton at the counter, ignore us as we enter. An 11 A.M. quiet fills the room.

On the wall by the door I read a large yellowed flyer dated 1910. It announces "only $45.50 an Acre" for the coming city of Southwestern Idaho. Now, more than eighty years later, the whole town of opportunity, all 40 acres, is on the block for $135,000.

I nose around the room, sizing it up as a potential homesite. The sepia walls could use some paint. I might keep the mounted animal heads—they add a nice primitive quality—but the shellacked buffalo clocks and animal-skin paintings have to go.

Red and green lights on a string of miniature Budweiser cans flash on and off over the bar. The bartender sees me staring at them. "My wife got those December 15, two years ago," he volunteers. "It's been Christmas around here ever since."

"Used to have blood pressure problems," he continues, moving unsolicited into his sales pitch, "but not since I came out here. Sometimes you see two cars go by at one time. Sometimes one in each direction. But that's kinda unusual."

I notice my family has gone outside and I head for the door. He calls after me, "If your friends left you, we can sure use the help."

How many times have I considered that offer? A new home, a fresh start. Grasmere, Idaho. Land of dreams, Town for Sale.

Odyssey

THE FARM CRISIS of the eighties hit the sheep industry hard, forcing many families out of the business. To save our own operation, we reassessed the costs of birthing our 5,000 ewes in midwinter in sheds along the Snake River in Idaho. It was a time-honored process but it demanded a lot in labor, feed, facilities, and time.

A neighbor trucked his sheep to Blythe, California, where his animals grazed and lambed on dormant alfalfa fields in warm weather. We were intrigued by the idea and spent many afternoons talking to him, penciling out the numbers, and weighing the options: trucking fees for the trip versus the high cost of feed for animals wintering in snow-covered Idaho; earlier lambs birthing in California versus cold weather deaths birthing in Idaho. The California option meant the simplicity of turning the ewes onto large alfalfa pastures where they would lamb and care for their newborn as they dropped. We would need only the one herder to stay with each band and portable fencing to keep the animals from straying.

Our decision in 1984 to give this a try was momentous in itself, but little did we realize we would begin a five-year odyssey traveling the back-country roads of the West in search of just the right place for this winter lambing to occur.

We were optimistic as we set off in our pickup that fall. We were looking for desert pasture or alfalfa fields that farmers leave idle in the winter and on which they usually are happy to have grazing sheep.

Our first stop was Pahrump, Nevada, a town whose name was severely ridiculed by my friends. "You're going where?" they howled in laughter. In those years, Pahrump, only 50 miles from Las Vegas, had not yet been discovered by developers and snowbirds fleeing cold climates. The town sat forlornly at the edge of Death Valley in scrub desert that reached out flat and empty toward faraway bare mountains.

As it turned out, Pahrump's few alfalfa fields were too spare for our sheep numbers and we moved on—south through Needles, California, south through Parker, Arizona, along roads choked by motor homes edging cautiously toward warm days. We stopped in each town to ask about pasture, spending an hour, sometimes an afternoon, talking to the biggest farm operators in the area. Wherever we drove, our eyes scanned the landscape to size up the possibilities.

We turned west at Quartzsite and rode the interstate to Blythe, where we checked into a pleasant-looking motel. But from its small bathroom window we saw the backside of town—of many rural southern California towns—a tiny shack in a dusty yard, a lone cactus, scattered plastic toys, ripped clothes on a line, a farm worker's family trying to survive. Several irascible roosters kicked up dirt and shattered the morning stillness each day.

We had been given the name of a man in Blythe who, we were told, was the middleman for all the alfalfa growers in the area. His office seemed to be a booth at Jerry's coffee shop, where over watery cups of coffee and tasteless processed food, we tried to get a straight story from him about the grazing prospects.

"There's lots of feed around here," he told us. We brightened up. "Lots of sheep too," he added. We slumped back into the plastic bench seat.

After several days of driving around the Blythe countryside seeing lush alfalfa fields already full of grazing sheep, we gave up. We headed farther south and west to Brawley across a silent desert road that heaved up and down through a roller-coaster succession of washes.

Several hours later we arrived at the home of the man described as the "godfather"—the unchallenged broker of pasture—in California's Imperial Valley. From the dimly lit living room of his old farm with large pieces of old furniture and tabletops cluttered with family pictures, we looked out at miles of flat, irrigated, green farmland and listened to his gloomy counsel.

"Gotta get the sheep off the alfalfa after the first rains," he warned, "even if the ewes are still lambing. It can be a mess and a real problem. The alfalfa growers don't want the sheep leaving tracks in their fields, you know."

We left shaking our heads. Brawley was only a short distance from the Mexican border, too many truck miles from Idaho, we rationalized.

We turned north and west toward the Bakersfield area and the Carrizo Plains. We met a sheep man at a coffee shop in Indio who claimed to have a fix on the entire Bakersfield-to-Riverside area. But it took only a cup of coffee to learn that he was in financial trouble. We had been warned. He was a hustler in the business of alfalfa fields.

Driving through the Tehachapi Hills later that day, we were struck with the brilliant greenness of the place after a first fall rain. On a whim, we pulled off the highway onto a "No Services" side road and followed it to a ranch house about a half mile away. The owners were generous with their time and our questions, but while my husband talked pastures with the owner, I was left to listen to his wife moaning about the future. "It's not worth staying in the livestock business," she whined. "Everyone's eating chicken. I tell him we're crazy to run cattle. It's a dead end for us." I brooded over her words all the way to Bakersfield.

"Foot rot," they told us as we drove through central California fields. "The fog's real bad in the winter and sheep come down with foot rot in the dampness."

My husband and I looked at each other. It was time to go home. Two weeks on the road had taken its toll. We longed for our own bed and a home-cooked meal. But as we headed north, we realized we had no idea what we would do with the sheep due to begin lambing in only eight weeks.

We continued by telephone to track the pastures of the West. My husband spent hours calling people we had met, following up leads—our journey went on from home.

"No," sighed our Blythe contact. "The pasture I told you about is taken after all, but try George. Something may have come up around Needles." Around and around we traveled by phone. I'm not sure which call led us to Bass Aja in Buckeye, Arizona, but suddenly there was a breakthrough.

Within days Bass put things in place and we were back in the pickup headed south to check on the desert country of the Harquahalla Valley, 70 miles west of Phoenix.

This part of Arizona can only be described as lonesome. The few inhabited homes looked forgotten in the empty space of abandoned farmland and desert brush. The country had been vacated after the aquifer dried up, cutting off the ready supply of water. The grasses looked good but only because it had been an unusually rainy fall.

There were the barest of services in a long low building that resembled a trading post and rambled inside from bar to sparse general store. The adjoining gas station was unhurried. Its owner seldom saw the nearby interstate business he had once anticipated. The station's hydrant turned out to be the only source of water in the area and the place we filled our water trucks every day for the sheep troughs several miles away. But, despite its bleakness, the Harquahalla Valley just might work for us, we decided, and we returned to Idaho to ready the crew.

In early December we loaded pickups and several herders and began the move to Arizona in time to unload the sheep trucks coming from our ranch headquarters.

We left Idaho in an angry snowstorm and crept along the straight and almost deserted icy Nevada highway through one terrifying whiteout after another. I drove our pickup white-knuckled most of the time with the herder Domingo in the passenger seat. He spoke no English. It was a quiet trip.

My husband followed close behind in the ranch truck that we would leave in Arizona for the winter. Our camp-tender, Jose Luis, rode with him. The storm finally wore itself out six hours later just north of Ely. At a gas station in that town, on the hood of the pickup, we spread out a map of the United States for the herders and with a finger, traced our route from the ranch headquarters south through Wells, Nevada, through Ely, and down the page until we stopped in an empty space we knew to be the Harquahalla Valley. This is where we are going, we explained—information that elicited a string of whistles and whoas from our two impressed passengers.

For almost a week my husband and I stayed at the closest motel to the sheep camps we could find, but it was in the Phoenix suburbs over an hour away. At the supermarket, we stocked up on onions, potatoes, meats, soap, and other supplies for the herders, and daily made the long trip back and forth from the suburb site through the desert to the camps.

The trip remains vivid to me even today. A drive through endless scrubbrush landscape broken only by a solitary nuclear plant and a surrealistic string of green road signs. The numbered markers counted off streets of the future, a curious extension of downtown Phoenix: 180th Street, 243rd Street, 290th Street. A developer's desert dream made real by a string of green signs planted in the sand. If only they could get water out here.

And water was the problem. That year the grasses were good because of the heavy fall rains but we couldn't count on the feed. In March as we loaded the sheep onto the trucks for Idaho, we knew this was only a temporary site and our odyssey to find the right place for the sheep would continue.

The second winter, we moved our four bands of sheep to pastures outside of Visalia, California. But the sheep man, our contact there, was rough on the animals and on our herders and that too became a one-winter stop.

A phone call to Needles, California, in the summer of 1986 proved a real breakthrough and we landed both feet and many hooves along the Colorado River in the Mojave Valley—an isolated 20-mile stretch of land belonging to the Colorado River Indian Tribes. They farmed the ground themselves or leased it to local growers.

For the next four years, Needles, often distinguished as America's hottest city in the summertime, became familiar country. In the winter the valley could be blissfully warm on still days or piercingly cold if the wind whipped down from the high mountain country to the north.

Needles was a service center, an all-American town, a way station along an empty stretch of interstate. Its downtown had a lazy, forgotten feel to it with neighborhoods reminiscent of depression days in the 1930s. The streets were lined with clusters of palms, orange trees, and neighborhoods of worn-out housing in dusty lots. Up on the rim, above the fray, were sleek 1950s-style homes. There were several great Mexican restaurants in town.

On the edge of Needles you drove across the Colorado River—and a time zone—to get to the farm valley where we wintered the sheep, five minutes away, or rather an hour and five minutes away. It was alfalfa and cotton country. Huge bales of tufted white cotton stacked along the highway served as landmarks for dirt road cutoffs through squares of cropland.

The valley stretched north of Needles until it ran headlong into the new city of Bullhead, a town 15 miles north exploding with trailer parks, condominiums, and shopping centers for wintertime residents. Bullhead looked out over the Colorado and into the glaring neon of Laughlin, Nevada, billed as the next Las Vegas and developing fast enough to live up to this moniker. Hotels ran regular passenger ferryboats from cars parked in Bullhead to casinos across the river. But this stretch of activity was another world from the quiet pastures where our sheep grazed.

Our herders stayed in an isolated trailer hidden in tall grasses and brush near the river. Often I'd climb through the thick underbrush to the shoreline and stare at miles of meandering water.

At Needles I made Christmas dinner one year for all the herders, an event later replaced by a wild night off in Laughlin. The men chose to celebrate the holiday at the brightest neon-lit hotel, and, for a mere $3.95 per herder, they settled into rapturous joy, returning again and again to the all-you-can-eat table. It was Christmas after all.

A young alfalfa producer subleased his fields to us the fourth year we wintered in the area. He offered the trailer behind his house to my husband and me when we came to check on the lambs, and it was there on New Year's Eve that we welcomed 1989 with champagne sipped from jelly jars from the trailer kitchen.

We had been in Needles only four years when farmers began to talk about land investment opportunities coming with the rapid growth of Laughlin and Bullhead City. In Idaho, my husband and I worried that our days along the Colorado River were numbered.

That spring of '89, a sheep man from Madera, California, told us he had pastureland and could handle our sheep numbers. We jumped at the opportunity.

Today we are settled with our animals grazing and lambing on fields along Interstate 99 in the heart of the San Joaquin Valley. The landscape is abundant with orange, almond, and pistachio trees and of course alfalfa that extends flat and far into the horizon. It is a prosperous area but only lightly populated. Still rural farm country. Ben Elgorriaga and his family, who run the sheep for us, have become friends. We wander through the Panoche Hills off Interstate 5 that have been home to his family and headquarters for their sheep operation for several generations. And as we walk through the warm, green California countryside, rarely do we think about icy-cold winters in lambing sheds along the Snake River.

Ranch Dogs

THERE IS A STRANGE BOND between humans and dogs that goes beyond words and rational explanations. I never fully understood this until I moved from the city onto the ranch.

There were dogs everywhere, most of them stock dogs that herded cattle with the cowboys or lived with the sheep in the mountains. For my husband there was Lucky, a dingo who stayed at the ranch in the winter to help the men with the cattle. But each spring, as soon as my husband's pickup appeared on the road, Lucky would greet its driver with delirious yelping and leaping. He and my husband were devoted to each other and spent hours driving the backroads around the ranch.

But one fall when we were getting ready for a three-week trip, Lucky moped around. He had seen us pack and unpack all summer but somehow he sensed a longer departure—maybe even winter. When we returned, Lucky had disappeared. Nothing brought him back. No rewards, appeals over the radio, calls to neighbors, none of the hours looking for him down backroads. He was still a young dog and years later, I continue to wonder what happened to him that faraway fall season.

For our wedding a year later, my parents gave us a black and white Border collie puppy. He grew into a healthy, loving animal who learned quickly, was good with the cattle, and loved us fervently.

He astonished us when we lost him in an unfamiliar southern Idaho town on a hot summer day. While my husband retraced his route, driving the streets and going from farm to farm looking for him, the dog found his way 20 miles north to our winter headquarters across freeways, through two towns, to arrive there before my husband. How he found his way through that unfamiliar country is still a source of amazement to us.

My husband tells many stories of ranch dogs but his favorite is about a smart sheepdog who, like so many others, roamed the hills with its herder. One morning as the band of sheep was coming off the desert, the herder and his dogs steered the animals through the outskirts of Carey. This was tricky because many of the houses are without fences, and the sheep, lured by the feed, can easily wander into fields of green grasses and alfalfa. Here the herders depend on the dogs to bring back the strays.

That night when the band arrived at the ranch, the herder noticed his best dog was missing. He waited all night for the animal to return and headed out the next morning to look for him.

He found the animal at the last place he had seen him, lying in the shade of some sagebrush. Next to him was the abandoned rock basement of an old house filled with a dozen sheep who were trapped in the pit. The dog had sat for twenty-four hours without food or water waiting for help.

"You can't train an animal to do that," my husband explained. "He knew there was trouble and waited for help no matter how long it took."

It seems impossible I knew so little about these amazing animals and how their relationship with livestock has evolved over thousands of years. Now I watch them sit in a pickup for hours just for a chance to gather the cows or watch over strays. And with us, they will hover at our feet for a stroke through their thick fur and go almost anywhere, if we are there. What an extraordinary experience I missed all those years alone.

Western Cafés

I LOVE SMALL-TOWN CAFÉS, and Connors, just off the interstate in southern Idaho, is one of my favorites. Recently, only after a hearty portion of eggs, hotcakes, and country sausage did I feel safe to scan the famous pie list hanging above the counter: apple, banana, custard, chocolate, French apple, berry, lemon, peach, butterscotch, and of course their famous oatmeal, a close cousin in taste to pecan.

The first Mrs. Connors, long since passed away, used to cook for sheep camps before she opened her own place. The current Mrs. Connors worked here five years before marrying the owner's son. Now her grown kids run the place with her. "Three generations," she announced proudly, flipping a hotcake on the grill.

In the middle of the front room is the locals' table, filled even on Sunday. The table is a sign of a good western café. When my husband and I travel the backroads of the West, we always stop at places like Connors. They all have a locals' table.

You don't have to be a farmer or rancher to find the café, but you should be one if you want to join the table. The men, dressed in jeans, flannel shirts, boots, and caps or cowboy hats, start arriving after morning chores, usually around 7 A.M. For the rest of the day, the table and the coffee cups are always full.

There's not much eating here—the wife at home handles that—but there's plenty of watery black coffee to go around. There is shop talk about the weather and the crops and some poking fun at each other. A few men leave, new ones arrive, the conversation begins again. No place for women at this table.

Food at these cafés is standard home cooking. At breakfast they have homemade biscuits, country gravy, and eggs anyway you like 'em. There are hamburgers all day long and always a pot of homemade soup. In the late afternoon you can stop by for pie made fresh that day and more coffee. Sunday dinner, after church, you can bring the wife for some roast turkey with gravy and mashed potatoes.

There's no better place to stop than these cafés when you're on the road. It's guaranteed the food, the talk, and the people are as western as the miles of sagebrush just outside of town.

Owls

WE WERE STARTLED by the noise above us and my husband and I looked up to see the outline of an owl against the night sky. It was large in its closeness as it swooped between the spruce tree in the front yard to the cottonwoods along the creek behind our cabin.

We had been standing in the dark listening to him call out in the warm fall evening, whoo, whoo, whoo. Now that he was in the cottonwoods, a second joined in, then a third owl, and in the chorus, my husband next to me. The night was alive with the distinctive whoo, whoo, whoo, the hoot of the bird Blackfeet Indians call "Ears Far Apart."

We sat under a sky full of stars and a pale slice of moon floating low in the sky and in this scene I remembered suddenly the small owl we had tried to save years earlier.

We found the bird huddled next to the back wall of the log cabin in the early spring. It was weak. "It must have fallen from the nest," my husband said. "Or maybe it was abandoned."

We brought the small creature finely shredded scraps of meat, careful not to touch him or leave our scent, hoping his mother would reclaim him. Days went by and he never moved. He seemed to be growing weaker.

Finally we realized his mother was not coming back and we began to bring him into the house to feed him. He did not resist our handling. I remember how large and wild he looked perched on the kitchen counter. He was beautiful. We thumbed the pages of *Audubon's Western Birds* and *Peterson's Field Guide* but he was so young we couldn't tell what kind of owl he was.

It was difficult to watch him grow weaker and weaker until one night he stopped taking food altogether. We decided to call the vet the next day, but in the morning when my husband went to find him in the bed of leaves behind the house, the bird had given up his struggle.

It haunted me for months and haunts me again tonight as I watch these owls soar overhead, calling to the others in the trees around the house. Living on the land, the cycles of life and death seem more closely bound together than anywhere else.

But for every lost lamb or bird I mourn, my husband points out new life. Lambs, colts, and calves rolling in green grasses. Nests of squeaking birds around our cabin, young antelope running in the hills, puppies falling over each other at the sheep camps, young owls waiting for night in the cottonwoods behind our house.

And this cycle of life tracks the seasons of the year, giving meaning to the vast space around me as we move forward, always forward, hoping for a better year, more rain, full crops, healthy animals. Now, in the silence of this night, I study the pale moon and the stars waiting to see an owl, to hear another and another.

Generations

I MET SCOTT one quiet Sunday afternoon when he came to our ranch headquarters. He drove up as I was walking to my cabin and asked if he could go to the gravesite of Jim Laidlaw. He told me Mr. Laidlaw had been his grandfather.

When I got back to the house, Scott and my husband were deep in conversation retelling stories Scott had heard from his mother. She was raised in this cabin. Scott sighed wistfully as he looked around the open space, brown and yellow in the warm midautumn day, and said, "I've never lived here but driving up the road, I know I have it in my blood."

Earlier that day I had been thinking about the three generations of families who have lived and worked on this ranch since we bought the place from the Laidlaws. My husband's grandfather, John Thomas, was first. His daughter and only child, Mary, was the second generation.

Her father pulled her aside after her husband's tragic drowning in the Snake River and told her, "Daughter, you have to learn the business and save the ranch for your son." And she did, running it until the early 1960s, when my husband, and the third generation, took over the ranch. Three generations, John Thomas, Mary, and my husband, running Flat Top Sheep Company.

Today our son, Tom, is assuming more responsibility for the ranch. He sighed one day after returning from a college friend's wedding. "They're all making such good money," he told me. "I have to wonder if this is a mistake out here."

My heart seemed to stop when I heard him. It is a fear so many of us in agriculture know today—this tension between a love of our work and the land, and the realization that our children can provide better for their families in an urban job.

Last year Tom planted acres of wheat, barley, and canola seed, working late into the night, sleeping little throughout the spring. He watched over the rows of shoots as they grew to full crops, then stood by helplessly as an unexpected hailstorm and early frost destroyed most of them. Fields of crops turned bad, nothing to sell for all his work, little left but feed for the cattle. A bitter harvest.

Recently when I went to Tom's house, I saw two chairs pulled to the edge of the porch where he and his wife must have sat the night before watching the evening sun spread across the hillsides where the cattle grazed. Or perhaps they sat there in the morning with steaming cups of coffee watching the light fill up the quiet space. And I saw in those two chairs a sign of hope beyond loss, of a love of place that is greater than money, and a deep commitment that passes like a poem from one generation to the next.

Waiting

THE LIGHT-COLORED HOSPITAL WALLS seem dull in the early-evening light. The building is hushed, but it is Sunday and it always seems quieter on Sunday.

We are waiting. My husband, our son, Tom, and daughter-in-law, Diane, and I are all waiting for Jacob to be born. But Jacob seems in no hurry to leave Diane and enter the world. And so we watch the light drain from the sky outside the window, turning hopefully from time to time to the expectant mother who simply shrugs. Waiting.

The low mumble of football on the elevated television fills in between our idle comments. We glance at it and then at Diane, then back to the bright images running and collapsing across the screen. Waiting. The fetal monitor machine rolls with the heartbeat, regular little bumps of Jacob's heart. Diane flushes every four or five minutes now.

Soon their eleven-year-old son Cory arrives with Diane's sister, her husband, and their young children, more family. Waiting. In today's world waiting is a terrible chore, an inconvenience, a kind of punishment or penalty. It often startles me into uncommon reflections. But tonight, instead, I think of all the times I wait.

When I first moved to the ranch, I quickly learned that my husband seemed to lose all track of time when he was working the cattle or fixing fence. "I'll be back at lunch," he'd call as he pulled away in his pickup. At noon I'd be ready with a meal, but waiting filled my lunch hours in those early days as the soup boiled away on the stove. Finally I learned eating at 2 P.M. was not all bad.

Whenever we drive around the ranch looking at young crops or checking the cattle, we stop at each gate, not simply to open it and drive through, but to wait while my husband wrestles with sagging fence line. The dog and

I watch the cloud patterns move across the sky, a hawk dive above a field. We tilt our heads to the call of a sandhill crane. Waiting for the repair. Waiting to drive on.

The contractions come more frequently now, every three minutes. Baby Jacob, our Thanksgiving child, we are waiting.

Then there are those cattle drives when rain forces us to hold over an extra day on the desert in the small cow camp. I cook a stew, the men play cards. We tell stories under the Coleman lantern hanging from the ceiling to brighten the gray day. Waiting for a break in the weather.

Or there was Christmas Eve in 1982 when I waited for my husband and his two sons during the big snowstorm. Four women—wives, a daughter, a mother—waiting for the men while they fought their way into the ranch, clearing the road with a Caterpillar, carving a path through the snow to feed the animals, save the livestock. They knew the blizzard was too much for our cowboy to handle alone. And we women waited at home, watching the telephone, the television, and the snow falling relentlessly outside the window. Waiting in the silence of a Christmas delayed. We talked in hushed tones as we do tonight in this hospital room, Diane and Tom now in the birthing room.

We wait, look at the clock, and wait. Then, with a raging howl, Jacob cries out. The waiting is over and the world sings.

Moving to Town

EVERY FALL IT HAPPENS at our ranch after the yellow leaves have fallen to the ground leaving the giant cottonwoods in winter nakedness. After the flowers hanging in pots from the eaves of the cabin have frozen in form on tall brown stems. After the families of our ranch hands have left this faraway headquarters for town so their children can go to school. After the wave of hunters stop coming by for coffee before they disappear into the hills around us. After a silence has settled over the land. Then the snows come, isolating us from town, and we must move.

First the livestock leave in caravans of stock trucks from Idaho to warm winter pastures in central California. There is an urgency to get them ready for the trip in those short, chill days of late fall. Some calves are sent to feedlots. Cows and heifers are vaccinated to help them produce healthy young. Others are retagged and recorded with red, green, or white plastic pieces pierced into ears like gaudy earrings. Then, in the first thin light of day, with frost snapping underfoot, the animals are loaded on trucks—the sheep loaded separately for a different destination—and they head for California to fatten and have their young.

After the animals are gone, we stack wood, pack away clothes and bedding to protect them from nesting mice, lock up equipment, and load pickups for cowboys moving out. Suddenly it is quiet.

My husband and I are the last to leave because we love it at this ranch so far from town. In the evenings we sit by the large, black woodstove in the kitchen, our source of heat, and fill ourselves with soup or stew simmering on its surface. We clean up mail stacked on our desks and sort through old magazines. But when the snow flies again, the 24-mile road to town will become too difficult to keep cleared, and the pipes at our uninsulated cabin will have to be drained.

Then we will leave this place of vast space, tall grasses, and sage-covered hills, of roaming antelope and birdsong, of creeks with fish for the taking, this place of quiet where we can breathe deeply of earth and sky. Reluctantly, we will pack up and move to town.

Winter

IN THIS SEASON *we are nomads. We store those items that can survive freezing temperatures, pack up the rest, and leave our uninsulated summer ranch headquarters for warm housing in town. We take to the road, driving long distances through the West to tend the cattle at the edge of our desert, and sheep in balmy California. At home we sit by the fire, snow covering our landscape, and read away the long dark nights. By day this is the season of quiet repair. The sun scatters diamonds across the snow while beneath its cover roads and fields heal themselves in the still-ness of this season. Game forage across wild lands. They dream of spring and so do we.*

Winter at the Ranch

IT IS DARK WHEN WE DRIVE into the snow country of Camas Prairie, but bright Christmas lights on farmhouses make the landscape seem warm and safe. The smell from wood-burning stoves fills the night air. The miles of open country white in the moonlight and stillness seem the way winter should be. And I think about our ranch.

Everyone's gone. Families have moved to town to be near schools. Several cowboys and the herders are in California tending the cattle and sheep grazing on winter pastures. The houses are boarded up. Snows have blocked the roads.

But there was a time when the ranch was busy all year. And I wonder, what it would have been like to spend this season at the end of a 24-mile deserted road with my husband, a team of horses, a bobsled, and 350 pregnant cows that needed tending while they calved and needed hay until spring thaws exposed the grasses?

When I first moved to Idaho, our cowboy Max and his wife Nola wintered at the ranch. They lived in the cook shack. It was the one building on the place that was insulated, but even so straw bales were pushed against the outside foundation to keep out the bitter cold. The county plowed the road to our gate after severe storms so that the couple could get to town every two weeks or so for supplies. The rest of the time the two of them simply holed up, taking care of the cows.

We called them every day and drove out to see them often during the winter, checking first to see if they needed anything from town. The drive was quiet. The snow piled up along the side of the road could be 10 feet high or more.

When we'd get there, Nola always had soup and coffee to warm us. She'd show me her latest project—crewelwork, crocheting, or painting. I'd watch her twist brown and orange yarns into a long afghan trailing off the edge of her lap onto the floor.

One Christmas season, we went to the ranch and Nola was addressing cards she had made. There was the delicious smell of cookies baking.

My husband and Max talked about the cattle, the hay, the weather. The small black-and-white television, pushed back in the corner, silently flashed snowy football images against the wall. We headed outside to look at the cattle and count the remaining hay bales in the shed to make sure there was enough for the weeks ahead.

On each trip my husband would reminisce about the time he wintered in the quiet and snow. That was before his legislative demands as a state senator kept him from the ranch from January through March.

"I can remember clear, cold mornings when the air was so still you'd hear Jim Mecham talking to his team of horses at his place five miles away. You don't know what quiet is until you feel something like that."

I'd close my eyes and listen for the "gee" and "haw," right and left directions, called into the icy air to the powerful horses pulling the hayrack through deep snows.

"It was different then," he went on. "You didn't feed with trucks. You'd get up on cold mornings, hitch the team to the sleigh, load it with hay bales, and pull out into the fields of cattle. When you'd feed, you'd drop flakes of hay in a circle so the timid animals got a chance at a second helping that hadn't been walked on. You'd sweep the sleigh rack clean so the cattle got the fine stems.

"When you pulled back to the barn, you'd park the sleigh on poles to keep the steel runners from freezing to the snow," he continued. "You'd leave the scoop shovel standing so you could find it in the morning if it snowed. And at night, you'd take the bridles inside so the bits wouldn't be too cold for the horses' mouths next day."

Small details that filled up a season, that saved lives, that made the ranch run. Could I have done it? I wonder.

I love listening to my husband tell his stories. We are not young, the two of us, but not old enough to have the past seem so long ago. Still, in a blink, today becomes the old days. It is simply because this life on the land is changing so quickly.

Several years ago, we gave up wintering at the ranch and sent the cows to California each November. This was a short-lived experience. Today the animals calve in Idaho again, but now at Kimama, on the edge of the Snake River Plain, 70 miles south of our summer ranch headquarters. We experiment constantly, looking for better ways to do business.

Although long since abandoned, the winter days at the ranch continue to hold the greatest mystery for me. Could I have done it? All that hard work in the punishing cold, work that could not be postponed when animals depended on feed brought in every morning. The silence, the remoteness, the storms. Would I have been lonely, or would it have been the solitude I often long for?

As we drive through quiet Idaho towns this snowy Christmas season, I know I am too late to live this cowboy life and am left with only the stories.

Snow

AT LAST IT HAS HAPPENED. After seven years of drought, there is moisture this winter. Not a little snow to ease us through the idea after years without. Not even moderate snow to begin filling our reservoirs again after they have been small pools for so long. But a reckless abundance, a deluge of snow, comes from the skies.

And our fragile earth, weakened after years of deprivation, seems unable to cope with the mountains of white that line our roads, threaten our roofs, paralyze our communities. The accumulation is unlike anything I can remember from the years before the drought.

Two days ago we got a call from a friend. Had we heard the roof had collapsed at a Bellevue stable and an avalanche had covered a living room in Hailey? We struggled with these images. Then, close to midnight, we received a call from a friend in Carey. He had snowmobiled into our ranch headquarters, close enough to report that a shed roof had collapsed and the snow was piling up precariously on the other buildings.

The urgency began. We knew we couldn't get in with men until the road was plowed. But we learned from county officials that they couldn't plow the 24 miles to our ranch until they opened the road to Magic Reservoir where some valley residents had been stranded for five days.

So we paced and worried, waiting for word that we could drive up the long, white, silent tracts to our headquarters. Then my husband, with our ranch hands, could begin to clear the roofs—on the barns, the shop, the garages, the homes, the work sheds. It would be hard, urgent work.

It seemed odd that winter came so indiscreetly. That after seven years of whispered promises, snows finally arrived in raging excess. And I wondered at the irony, as one crisis led to another, whom to believe. Whom to hold responsible. I read claims that decades of industrial abuse have disrupted weather patterns irrevocably. But perhaps it was just a capricious God testing our stamina and determination to love this land.

Christmas in Carey

CHRISTMAS STORIES. They are everywhere. But then I love Christmas. As a child, I was in a state of high agitation from the day Santa arrived at Macy's Thanksgiving Day Parade in New York until well after New Year's Day. And today, just like when I was five, I am warmed by the small colored lights that transform ordinary houses and shops into places of magic. I sing along recklessly with carols that float through the background of my days and insist that my home smell of freshly cut greens and baking cookies the month of December.

Now I realize that not all people are afflicted with this Christmas delirium, so I try to subdue myself. But when I least expect it, I am brought back to the mystery of the season.

Like last week. My husband and I drove through our small hometown of Carey on the way to the ranch. We were retrieving several items before the big snows come and close the road.

But I was struck that in the pale light of late afternoon, this rural town looked tired. Its buildings, many in need of paint, seemed to wear the hard work of its people. The struggle of these family farmers spilled out across the lonely winter landscape like wild grasses across vacant lots.

I tried hard to remember the busy farm town of summer, the dusty pickups parked around the sports shop, the cars and campers on their way to Yellowstone squeezed around gas pumps at Adamsons, the fairgrounds crowded with people and livestock, pets, the parades and picnics, the rodeo. It had only been several months, but this Sunday it seemed years ago. Streets were deserted, stores were closed, neighbors stayed home by the fire after morning chores. Silence tiptoed across the fairground lawn.

And so I was taken aback several hours later when we returned after dark. The first farmhouses we passed caught our attention with a startling

Christmas brightness. The porch of one home was strung with yellow, red, and green bulbs; trees around a second farm were threaded with white lights that danced on and off.

As we got closer to town, the number of decorations seemed to swell until we turned onto Main Street and into a blaze of light and color, none of it visible in the earlier gray daylight. There were roofs outlined in flashing bulbs, candles in windows, yards filled with lighted trees.

Strings of white outlined reindeer pulling Santa and his sleigh across a front porch, a green wreath with a huge red bow lighted up a building wall, a number of families had framed windows in colored lights to show off plump Christmas trees inside. And of course, there were lighted nativities outside the several small churches in town.

It was enough magic to impress the most cynical. I realized that earlier in the gray afternoon, I had forgotten about the tenacity of our neighbors in this quiet farm town. It took the mystery of darkness and the miracle of Christmas for their hope and determination to be fully revealed.

Sheep in the Basement

THE STRANGE CALL came as my husband and I were dressing to go to a Christmas party. I listened, confused at first, to the Forest Service employee on the phone. "There is a sheep [pause] in the basement [another pause] of a house in Sun Valley," he rushed to conclude. "A house on the fairways," he added again hesitantly, knowing this elegant address raised the prospect that any damage could be expensive.

I put my husband on the phone. The home owners had moved back to their house for the holidays to discover that the animal had jumped through the closed basement window. They didn't know how long it had been there. "I don't think it's our sheep," I heard my husband, who knows the area, say, "but I'll see what I can do." We canceled the Christmas party and changed into work clothes.

On the short drive from our winter apartment to the house, I tried to picture what had been described as "the basement," fingers crossed in hopes that it would be one of the concrete-floored, unfinished places with storage boxes shoved into dark corners. But as we drove up to the imposing house, my heart sank. I knew immediately that nothing here would be unfinished, not even a basement.

The owners opened the door and we recognized the couple right away. They greeted us politely, trying to subdue their anxiety. But as we followed them through their tiled foyer and tiptoed down the white carpeted stairs leading to "the basement," I knew the worst. The animal was behind the closed door at the bottom.

As we entered the room cautiously, I took in the rose-colored walls and a huge bed elevated high off the floor on a log bedstead. The mattress was covered by a mauve, floral bedspread. Next to it were a matching armchair and ottoman. Beyond, jagged shards of glass around the broken window framed the night sky. Then we came face-to-face with a very large ewe who wore the same confused expression I had already seen too many times this night.

On the floor, our friends had laid out a newspaper page like a placemat and placed a mound of granola, three lettuce leaves, and a carrot in the middle. Next to this was a plastic bucket of water. Clearly the concerned hosts were doing what they could against impossible odds.

Beyond the feeding ground, the very white carpet was a dreadful sight, covered with small brown pellets of sheep droppings. Here and there were spots of dried blood from the gashes in the ewe's legs.

I tried to console myself, as I scanned the room, that at least she had not gotten onto the bed, kicked holes in the walls, or rammed the antique wooden bureau and knocked the ceramic pieces onto the floor in mutilated pieces. Small blessings these. It was about this time I was willing to agree with my husband. This could not be our sheep. No sir, our sheep would never do this.

The couple told us about bear and cougar in the area, and we speculated that indeed something must have frightened the ewe and caused her to jump through the glass. Perhaps she saw her reflection in the window and sought the safety of another sheep. We'll never know for sure.

About that time, and much to my relief, two men arrived who had been summoned to pull up the carpet. They would be far more useful to my husband than I could be. Quickly the three of them harnessed the sheep, walked her up the white carpeted stairs now hastily covered with pale yellow-and-white-checked sheets, and lifted her into the back of our pickup. She seemed as eager to be gone as the rest of us were to get her out.

As we pulled out of the driveway, I noted the relief on the face of our friends. I tried to imagine the shock of coming upon such a huge animal rummaging through my lovely pink and lavender guest room—should I have such a place.

But then I cheered. After all, I thought, what better occasion to entertain sheep than Christmastime? That is, if you're going to entertain at all.

Christmas Journey

IT WAS CHRISTMAS DAY and things were different. You could feel it in the air. We were driving to California to check on our sheep lambing on warm winter pastures and we seemed alone in the world.

We had a family dinner on Christmas Eve with toasts to one another and with the love and warmth of the season spread across the table. The next morning we opened presents together around the tree with carols playing and breakfast sweets to nibble on. But by afternoon my husband and I were on the road pushing the open miles to Winnemucca.

As soon as we lost daylight, it became obvious that this was not just another day. Everything was so silent in the dark. There was no traffic, no people on the streets. Stores were closed.

A deep fog folded around us as we climbed through the Owyhee Mountains. We saw no other car on our climb, no faint headlights working the fog. The night was lonely.

In Jordan Valley, the last stop before the long stretch through the Oregon desert, only one gas station was still open at 7 P.M. Its attendant was huddled inside to stay warm. One hundred and one miles down the road, just over the Nevada border in McDermitt, the Say When Casino was dark. We stopped at a small gas station across the highway to make a call. Two women gossiped behind the counter under bright lights. We wished them Merry Christmas and pulled back onto the dark road.

When we reached Winnemucca, there was little room at the inn. Not because the town was full, but because innkeepers had closed up to celebrate Christmas with their families and friends. We finally found lodging and wearily headed for a hotel casino restaurant for a second chance on the day—a little turkey dinner, we hoped. What we found was leftover bird with gummy gravy plopped on top of dry meat. Our early start to

California seemed a bleak idea as we squinted to shut out the yellow-pink glare of casino light. Christmas and home were far away.

But the next morning, to our surprise, it was business as usual in this Nevada town. The holiday and our strange night were behind us.

That day we drove through Nevada desert, up and over Donner summit, and into the warm air of central California farm country. I played Christmas music most of the morning, unwilling to let go of this sweet time of year.

We reached Madera and joined our sheep manager midafternoon. "The ewes are lambing about fifty a day," Denny told us. "We're almost halfway through, much earlier than last year." This was good news.

We drove out to alfalfa fields and walked through ewes and the smallest lambs, many of them barely able to stand on wobbly legs. They tumbled over each other and staggered to their mothers' sides at the sight of strangers. In another field, lambs born several weeks earlier jumped and spun around under the watchful eyes of the wooly ewes.

This new life was a scene of absolute joy and promise. And the sight of these young lambs running free in the sunshine erased the loneliness of the day before and gave purpose to the long Christmas night drive.

Sheepherders' Christmas Feast

EVERY CHRISTMAS, I am reminded that the sight of shepherds with their flocks is not something that lives only in biblical passages but is part of my own Christmas at Flat Top Sheep Company ranch. It is that way if you worry over the fate of five bands of sheep, close to 5,000 wooly creatures, year-round.

The men who care for our animals, our herders, come from around the world. When I first moved here in 1981, most of them were from the Basque country of Spain, then Mexico, and more recently Peru. They spend the spring in the desert country and summer in the high mountains that make up parts of our ranch. But in the winter, men and animals settle on warm pastures in central California.

We drive down from Idaho over the Christmas holidays to see the operation, bringing holiday treats to the men in sheep camps. But there was a time when we took our animals to Arizona in the winter. And it was there, along a quiet stretch of the Colorado River in thick brush that framed flat farm country just across the bridge from Needles, California, that I remember most clearly a Christmas with the herders.

That year, when my husband and I made our annual holiday trek, I was overwhelmed with good cheer and decided that what the men really needed was a festive Christmas dinner, even on December 28. I could put it all together in their large trailer hidden away in the wild, tall grasses along the riverbank.

The men were not as enthusiastic as I was about this idea, especially when it became clear they had to clean their trailer and the confusion of pots and dishes nested in the kitchen sink before I could begin. I drove 15 miles north to a large supermarket at Bullhead City and returned with bags of Christmas foods. Only then was I told that the tap water was undrinkable. This lent a new dimension to cooking.

I had not finished processing this information when Jose Luis, our Spanish camp-tender, announced that he didn't like turkey. "Oh no, no, no," he shook his head violently. "But I will eat the potatoes and vegetables," he added generously.

Undaunted, I spent the day chopping, stuffing, basting, and mashing and when the herders came in that afternoon at 5, the small trailer smelled deeply of turkey and other baking foods. To my surprise, the men all showered and came to the table, hair freshly combed and with clean shirts on. It made the dinner seem like a real party.

I brought out the turkey and trimmings and watched aghast as Jose Luis promptly ate not one or two helpings of turkey, but four. I'd never seen anyone who didn't like turkey respond so well to this browned bird. "Not bad," he finally gasped between mouthfuls.

I watched the Peruvian herders, Raul, Paco, and Andreas, each bite into the sweet potatoes, a taste of home, and almost weep. The three of them went on to devour close to 10 pounds of sweet potatoes along with the turkey, stuffing, cranberries, and vegetables. It was an inspiring performance.

The next day, Jose Luis, who still claimed he *usually* didn't like turkey, ate three sandwiches of white meat stacked on dark for lunch. At the end of the table, Raul, Paco, and Andreas silently poked at the turkey carcass, bereft that there were no more sweet potatoes.

As a cook, I don't think I've ever felt as pleased with a meal. As a Christmas gift, it may have been my finest. Now we send the sheep to a permanent location outside of Madera and I bring Christmas cakes and breads because there is no central camp in which to gather and cook. Jose Luis has gone back to Spain and the Peruvians just look wistful when my husband and I drive up with packages. And I know Christmas will never again be quite as wonderful as turkey and sweet potatoes all together in the trailer in tall grasses along the Colorado River.

Digging Out of Christmas

It was two days after Christmas when I decided to join my husband on a drive into the ranch. That he had only three weeks earlier gone through hip replacement surgery and was still unable to bend over or put much weight on his right leg had some small part in my decision. But despite a wonderful holiday in town filled with family gatherings, food, carols, gifts, and music, on this warm, sunny day I was ready for the quiet landscape of the ranch. There was some snow on the road but our pickup could easily break trail through it, or so I thought.

It was several hours later as I crawled from underneath the truck, dragging the scoop shovel, my husband leaning on his cane and instructing me exactly where to heave the snow I had hauled out, that I began to reassess the wisdom of this trip. In all honesty, he had dug us 90 percent out of this snowdrift despite his unsteady condition. It's the cowboy way, don't you know. He stopped short at getting under the truck to clear the axle, instead assuring me that the long-handled scoop shovel would make short work of this job. Still, I found myself crawling under the vehicle to jab at the icy mound of snow.

And there, on my hands and knees, inexplicably I had an image of my sister, the one in Old Greenwich, Connecticut. The one who has become my best friend as we've grown older. The one who at that very minute was serving afternoon Christmas tea to several of her friends. I could see it clearly. She had had a similar tea last year when my husband and I were visiting family over the holidays.

When I was growing up, my family fully understood Christmas, and our house was filled with greenery, music, colored lights, and a huge tree decorated with many of the ornaments that had hung on my mother's tree when she was a young girl. Family always came to visit—grandparents, aunts, uncles, cousins.

And there was food. Wonderful treats from smoked fish to crocks of English Stilton cheese. There was a time when a wealthy family friend sent us a gift tin of caviar each year. We savored this delicacy on Christmas Eve on silver dollar–sized pancakes with minced onion, egg, and sour cream. Then there was roast goose and plum pudding for Christmas Day. I think my mother was seriously influenced by Charles Dickens.

Christmas morning, the four of us children were not allowed downstairs until my dad, in robe and slippers, checked the area for weasels. He had it on good authority, he warned us, that they ran through houses on Christmas Eve, nibbled on any foods left out, and even rummaged through holiday presents. But, he added, he would protect us.

So while we waited impatiently at the top of the stairs, we heard this otherwise serious man, completely out of character, stomping through the downstairs shrieking at the weasels to "go on, get out of here, scram." We were terrified of these critters and it gave him time to set up the camera and capture our expressions when we first entered the room and saw our presents.

At Christmastime we'd go into New York and stare open-mouthed at the huge tree at Rockefeller Center. We'd see the Rockettes at the Radio City Music Hall Christmas show and wander along Fifth Avenue peering at the magic winter scenes in department store windows. Dad would take us to lunch at a special restaurant with white tablecloths and napkins, then to FAO Schwarz to look at shelves of toys. Maybe we'd skate at the Rockefeller Center ice rink. But the day was never complete without a small bag of roasted chestnuts from a corner street vendor before we headed for Grand Central Station and the hour train ride home.

Christmas was magic growing up and even today I am still under its influence. Until last year's trip to Connecticut, I thought I was unnaturally obsessed by this holiday. But I'm a piker next to my sister, who treated us to the highlight of the season, afternoon tea. It was then I saw her house in Christmas dress for the first time. Every windowsill, shelf, fireplace mantle, and tabletop was filled with treasures, beautiful objects she had spent years gathering from antique shops—the perfect doll, santa, angel, village scene pieces. My sister's house was a small museum. "For the children," she explained as if I might believe this. "For the children," I laughed.

She served us tea because she loves high tea the way others love a night on the town. In new cities, she seeks out the restaurant or hotel that serves afternoon tea and goes there first, before the monuments, theater, and museums, to linger over delicate food morsels served on silver trays complemented by tea she lightens with milk. Violin music fills the room.

And when she serves tea for family and friends, it is no less elegant. Last Christmas, we nibbled cookie-sized sandwiches of cucumber, then smoked salmon, then turkey, crusts removed, and indulged on tiny cakes, cookies, fruit tarts, truffles, and dark chocolate mice. We sipped champagne, then tea. Greens perfumed the room.

But into this Christmas reverie came my husband's voice. "How ya doing under there?" I was pulled back to the axle in front of my face, the wet snow under my body, the snowdrift blocking the road, the one that looked flat in the late-afternoon light but wasn't. I was at the ranch again, stuck in the snow.

In the silence of this western landscape as the sun disappeared behind the ridge line, we finally broke free. Chilled but relieved, I settled into the pickup. And about that time, I knew that all I really wanted *right then* was a cup of tea.

Coco in Baja

MY HUSBAND AND I raised plastic cups in a toast to each other on December 30. It was the anniversary of our first meeting fifteen years ago when I was visiting the resort community of Sun Valley over Christmas.

But instead of the snow and holiday lights of the ski town, we sat under a bright three-quarter moon in the Baja Mexico desert wilderness. Our tent was nearby in the sand. The fire built against a wall of white boulders popped occasionally, breaking the stillness. Cacti surrounded us like sentinels in strange and lovely designs.

My husband and I stared into this landscape we have come to love over the years and toasted Coco, who had directed us to this wild and remote place.

Coco was the proprietor of an odd roadside attraction some miles away. We began to see his ragged signs that read "Coco's Ahead" almost as soon as we pulled off the north-south highway. We were determined to take the side road to the gulf coast bay of San Luis Gonzaga despite the route's rugged appearance. It was at an intersection of two primitive dirt roads that we found Coco's strange outpost and stopped out of curiosity.

It stood in glitter and confusion, a museum of memories. Strings of Tecate beer cans were cut and fluted into lantern shapes. They hung like flags strung from wires, reflecting sunlight across the sand. A small travel trailer, Coco's home, was covered with all manner of bumper stickers and decals. It was parked under a thatched roof that extended out to the road. Strange articles hung from the ribs of the roof or leaned against support poles—things like tire rims, inflatable beach toys, crutches, a surfboard, a bicycle, and a red highway stop sign. Folding metal chairs stenciled with Carta Blanca beer logos and vinyl cushions for visitors were scattered across the sandy floor.

Outside, a fire extinguisher hung from a lanky cactus branch and a plot of camotes, sweet potatoes, sent up vivid green shoots to cover the trellis next to the trailer. A sign above it all read "Coco's Corner. Tourist Info. Open."

Coco appeared as soon as we stopped the pickup. He was a large man in a faded pink shirt. His deep brown skin and bleached white hair had been colored by hours in the desert sun, a small ring of white beard outlined his chin.

We wandered with Coco as he pointed across wild lands into distant mountains and told us of hidden backroads. He could identify every car that passed that day and its direction. He answered questions about the desert, about his curious collection of memorabilia, and about a road grader behind the trailer that had caught my husband's eye. Coco used it, he said, to smooth the long stretch of dirt road from the gulf to the main highway. But not recently.

When he asked where we were going, we told him, "Bahia San Luis Gonzaga."

"No, no, no," he corrected. "Tomorrow, not today. Forget the gringos. Go to the desert." We liked this idea.

He told us about a road we would have missed without directions. "Follow it to mountains and the arroyo with water," he instructed. "It is beautiful back there. Forget the gringos," he called after us as we pulled away in the pickup.

We were happy to follow Coco's advice. And in the moonlight, from our remote and quiet campsite my husband and I toasted fifteen years together as we settled into the beauty of the desert landscape, and we toasted Coco and all those at home in remote and wild country.

Meling Ranch

"MY NAME IS AIDA," she stated simply, as though it were the most common of names. "Most people call me Ada but I prefer the real thing, Aida." I was caught off-guard by the grandeur of the name, known only to me from opera, and I certainly never expected to meet an Aida in the remote backcountry of northern Baja Mexico.

She was the matriarchal figure of the Meling family ranch, a sizable cattle operation in the brush country started by her grandfather over a hundred years ago. This operation is a union of the Johnsons and the Melings, Norwegian and Danish families. It is 31 miles, or an hour-and-a-half drive, down a deeply rutted dirt road off the main north-south Baja Highway.

At first, I was reluctant to spend time at a ranch on my Christmas vacation away from Idaho. I am hardly deprived of ranch experiences. And briefly, my eyes and mind wandered west of the highway, where I could glimpse long strands of isolated sandy beach. But instead my husband and I turned east to the mountains that form a spine down the length of the country. We were curious to see this historic Mexican ranch.

It was late afternoon and we passed several cars on their way into the small town of San Telmo, 8 miles from the highway. After that, early-winter darkness closed in around us and we found ourselves alone on the dirt road with only several rabbits that raced in front of our headlights.

The similarity between the drive into the Melings and that into our Idaho ranch was curious. In both cases we watched for rocks and ruts in the road, caught glimpses of scrub brush and sage in the truck's lights, and in the distance to the north and south felt the presence of rolling hills leading into mountains.

As we pulled up to the main house, we could see through the windows, under vine-covered arbors, ranch guests sitting down to dinner at long tables. We stepped out of the cold mountain night into a room warmed by a large fireplace.

Sonia, Aida's middle-aged daughter, met us at the door, and we were seated at the first of many enormous ranch meals with homemade bread, homemade jam, homemade salsa, frijoles and rice, vegetables from the large ranch garden, and whatever casserole suited the day. Sometimes eggs were brought in from town, Aida told us, because the ducks ate the chickens' eggs before the cook could get to them. "So," Aida shrugged, "maybe we'll just eat more duck."

Over the next two days we stayed at this Mexican mountain hideout, like John Grady Cole or Butch Cassidy, miles from main roads and telephones, where the generator was turned off at 9 P.M. except on New Year's Eve. Then, with guests and cowboys we danced Mexican polkas and toasted 1994, sharing bottles of beer, champagne, wine, and tequila, whatever anyone contributed to the evening.

Aida told us of growing up on this ranch. Her education alternated between a year with a tutor here and a year of school in the States. She told of family trips—four days by horse-drawn wagon—to Ensenada, now a five-hour drive. These trips for Aida were a treat because she could play with children at other ranches where they spent the night.

She told us the history of the buildings, that the large stone and wood-beamed dining room had burned to the ground during the 1911 Mexican Revolution but was rebuilt almost immediately as it is today. She told of her father who spent three months each year in the rugged desert interior of Baja gathering wild cows several hundred miles south of the ranch. The cattle's mouths were full of needles from the cactus they ate, she told us.

She showed us on a map the four ranches where today their livestock move and graze seasonally and pointed to the area where they are rounded up for branding and doctoring each spring.

Last year during the big rains, the family was cut off from town for over a month, Sonia told us, but with the supplies for guests, the two women were able to feed themselves and their neighbors the entire time.

Two hardy and self-sufficient women, mother and daughter, miles from the highway, from telephones, from supplies, running their grandfather's and great-grandfather's ranch. Two women who stood with us in front of the large fireplace, Mexican music filling the dining room on New Year's

Eve, glasses raised in a toast to wish the best for two ranch families, one from Mexico and one from Idaho.

Wool Markets

LAST CHRISTMAS, I made a wild stab at bringing my husband shopping with me. As I swooped over tables of sweaters and through racks of shirts and slacks, finding items perfect for our daughter and son, I realized my husband hadn't gotten past the clothing at the front of the shop. I went back to fetch him, only to find him reading labels. Our shopping trip was over.

"Look at this," he began. "Taiwan. Malaysia." He was waving sweaters in the air. "Here's one from China." I tried to get him to put down the merchandise and help me select gifts but his research project was quickly draining the fun from the day. We tried a second shop. It was the same. I should have known better than to expect help from him. But he was right.

In recent years, he has taken to reading labels in clothing shops. For him it is about the condition of workers in Third World countries paid $1 a day, working without health and environmental safeguards. It is about world trade. Who really wins as we expand our markets?

I understand his concern because it affects us all the way to our ranch. We have experienced the vagaries of international trade when countries like Australia and New Zealand support their sheep industry to boost its productivity and world trade opportunities. We are left to compete against these odds without the same support from our government.

This year, for the first time ever, we locked the door of our ranch shop on rows of the new, large 400-pound bags of wool, maybe 120 in all. They were stacked high in the large room, protected from rain and snow in an angry protest, our only statement against the desperately low prices we were offered.

We are not the only western sheep family who held on to our wool rather than sell it. Fifteen years ago it was worth as much as $1.15 per pound. In 1999, we were offered 18 cents—less than in the depression years and far less than it cost us to shear the animals in October.

Few of us in the industry understand these low prices. We are told the Australian Wool Board first hoarded its supply and now is dumping it on world markets. Then there are the effects of synthetic products. This year, as if to seal our fate, three large U.S. woolen mills closed their doors. But more than this, it seems to come back to the huge international corporations who play one country's workforce against another. We producers become pawns as they amass huge profits. It is the free market we are told, but my husband is skeptical. "I've had about all the freedom I can afford."

This year I saw an L.L. Bean Christmas catalog featuring sweaters of New Zealand wool. I threw the book away, realizing that around Idaho from Emmett to Soda Springs, we are forced to store our wool in a last protest.

At the Wool Growers' convention in November, buyers from around the region tried to persuade reluctant sheep men to sell, treating us as if we were bad children to hold out. But at 18 cents per pound, my husband suggested, the sacks of wool are more valuable to the ranch as windbreaks.

Is globalization of trade inevitable? It seems so as we read labels on clothing racks. But at what price? A world robbed of quality and human purpose? If globalization means we will lose rural America to international markets that provide no human rights or environmental safeguards, then I am left to wonder what really matters to any of us.

Basque Food

IF I'M SEEN HUFFING AND PUFFING at a health club these days, it is not only to work off the excesses of the holiday season. I am getting myself in shape for the Basque restaurants beckoning in garlic waves along roads between our Idaho ranch and the California fields where our sheep graze each winter.

My husband and I love Basque food and over the years we have sampled restaurants all over the West. We start the evening with a "picon punch" at the front bar. This bitter, ruby-colored drink can knock you flat if you're not ready for the first wicked sip.

In the crowded family-style dining room reminiscent of the early boardinghouse days, we are wedged into seats across from each other in the middle of a long table. We are next to strangers who will soon become friends as we pass the red wine and crusty white bread back and forth.

We are brought a small tureen of steaming soup that we ladle into bowls in front of us. Warmed by the savory blend, we scoop out a second helping, knowing we will regret this excess later in the meal. Then comes the garlic-laced salad. We bite into its cool tanginess. And without a breath come beans in thick red broth, crisp french fries, and side dishes of chorizo and chicken buried in saffron rice, or sweetbreads or tongue in rich brown gravy. Then the main course, the only dish we select. It will probably be lamb, our favorite, stewed, grilled, or roasted—we don't care. We take a deep breath as our server offers us flan or a scoop of ice cream for dessert. We can't move let alone lift a spoon.

We never tire of looking for new Basque restaurants or returning to our favorites, like The Martin in Winnemucca. Recently we struck up a conversation there with three Basque men from Elko. When we sat down, they were several glasses of red wine into lunch and happy to talk food. Anticipating a trip to the winter Cowboy Poetry Gathering in their hometown, we prodded them about local Basque establishments. "Go to The Star for steaks, the Nevada Club for lamb chops, and The Biltoki for their side dishes," one advised while his companions nodded in agreement.

We compared notes with them on Louis' and the Santa Fe in Reno, The Woolgrowers and The Chalet in Bakersfield, and my favorite, a Los Baños restaurant where a multicourse meal in the large, plain dining hall includes a large chunk of hard white cheese at the end.

You find the best Basque restaurants, like The Martin, across from the railroad tracks in western towns. The building is part bar, part dining room, and part boardinghouse/hotel used for years by Basque sheepherders when they came to town.

In some, the old wooden bar is the centerpiece of the building. In others it's the banquet rooms, formerly dance halls. These often have intricately designed tin-tiled ceilings and floors of flowered linoleum that look like a large embroidered rug. Back hallways lead past guest rooms. Walls everywhere are covered with yellowed photos of sheep camps, lambings, and herders at work. They are the stories of the sheep industry in the West.

It is hard to say whether we love these places for the small museums they are or for the multicourse, garlic-rich food they provide. But Basque restaurants are treasures to discover from Bakersfield to Boise, deliciously filling in our western landscape.

Hauling of the Bulls to California

DAY AFTER DAY, we watched the weather channel while it rained steadily in Idaho. The night before we were to haul four bulls to our cows in California, my mother-in-law greeted me at the front door. "They've had sixty inches of snow on Donner Summit in the last twenty-four hours," she announced, half thrilled, half terrified. But then she admitted that the snow had stopped, and we both knew that with my husband's indomitable spirit, the trip was on. If Donner was open, we would haul the bulls across its summit the next day. Very little could stop us crossing the most unpredictable yet heavily traveled mountain pass in the West.

By 6 A.M., my husband and I were in the pickup with our dog in the backseat. We were headed for Winnemucca. There we met our son at a truck stop on the edge of town. He arrived in the sturdiest of our ranch pickups pulling the horse trailer loaded with the four huge black animals. We traded vehicles and headed for the interstate and west. We lumbered along the highway in the slow lane. "We're pulling close to eight thousand pounds," my husband told me as I watched the wide-open Nevada countryside drag by the window. Every once in a while the bulls shifted in the back and we felt the rolling motion in the cab of the truck.

Just outside of Reno we began the anxious climb into the Sierras. We stopped at the California inspection station and I ducked across lines of traffic to get the health papers for the bulls stamped in the small office. Meanwhile, at the truck, my husband and the guard talked about the 400 inches of snow on Donner this year. When I returned, the two were shaking their heads at the promise of floods to come.

We found our place in the slow line of traffic between a string of long-haul trucks. The brightness of the white world and brilliant blue sky caused us to squint even behind sunglasses. Our ears exploded.

We climbed higher. The pickup groaned under the weight. We shifted down and down again as we stared at magnificent mountain peaks. At last we reached the summit.

Now we had to guard against runaway. In low gear we descended, counting out the elevation markers, 5,000, 4,000, 3,000, 2,000, then the straight haul into Sacramento and south onto Highway 99.

It was late by the time we pulled onto Route 4 outside of Stockton. The sky had lost all sign of color. I groped for a flashlight. It would be dark when we unloaded the bulls.

A half hour later we eased down the ranch dirt road, deeply rutted after days of rain. Rabbits darted in front of the headlights and out into the fields.

At the corrals, my husband walked the muddy lot with the flashlight before he backed the pickup and horse trailer through the gate to block the exit. Then we swung open the trailer door and bulls disappeared into the blackness of the corral.

We scattered flakes of hay around the pen for the animals, following the thin stream of handheld light. In the morning, our cowboy would turn the bulls into the green pastures with the cows.

Then the magic moment of freedom for us. We eased the pickup from the gate and unhitched the trailer. Like an albatross slipping from our necks, the pickup glided away from the leaden weight. It was late and we were tired and hungry. It had been our slowest trip from Idaho to these California pastures, but we had made it. And without snow. We headed down the ranch road, feeling free to settle into the exhaustion we had earned.

Elko Cowboy Poetry Gathering

THE ANNUAL COWBOY POETRY GATHERING is held in the coldest part of winter, just before calving starts on north country ranches. In these short days, cowboys and would-be cowboys, as many as 8,000 people, head to Elko in the heart of Nevada ranch country. They come to live out, or perhaps just reaffirm, the cowboy dream for several days. They read poems, trade stories, sing songs, dance till 5 A.M.

I missed the early years but now I am hooked. I stand against a display of handcrafted saddles and rawhide gear and try not to stare at the men walking by.

Buckaroos strut like peacocks, jeans tucked into boots of red, purple, navy with scarves of green, yellow, pink wrapped flamboyantly around their necks. They have mustaches twirled tight into curls or waxed thin into toothpick-fine extensions. And of course they wear hats—wide-brimmed, high-crowned, rounded, the bigger the better sitting atop fresh scrubbed young faces or pulled down over the ears of weathered old-timers. The fanciest women pale next to their partners.

There is good poetry and bad, but mostly it's sentimental. Each session beginning at 9 A.M. is jammed, attention riveted on the stage. And through-out the day, poets—cowboys, buckaroos, ranchers, and ranch wives—lead their audience down coulees and draws, up rimrock ridges, toward sunsets and starry nights riding the range on their sorrels or bays.

It is the Old West, camp cooks, brandings, and ropings painted vividly in verse that often moistens the eyes of the burliest men around me.

Recently a stranger challenged me, "You like that awful cowboy poetry." I counted to ten trying to subdue myself. Then I remembered that recently I heard one of the founders of the Elko gathering, a large, gentle man named Hal Cannon, speak about how he happened onto cowboy poetry.

His interest was in western culture, he explained. In its pursuit, he traveled the region visiting ranch families and soon discovered the unique role poetry played in the lives of so many cowboys. He was usually shown a family scrapbook sometimes brought down from a closet shelf or lying on the coffee table in the living room. These family collections were full of pictures, clippings, and scraps of poetry.

"I was fascinated," he said, "with this basic interest we all seem to have to create books."

He learned a lot about cowboy poetry on his travels. Cowboys and buckaroos told him they recited poems to stay awake when they were moving cattle or driving late at night from one rodeo to another. Others told him it was a lot easier reciting poems to a girl you met in a bar than trying to talk to her. And still others told him about the game of reciting poems while playing cards. The first one to forget a line buys a round of drinks.

Hal and some cowboy friends decided to bring these poets together to share their words. Before the first gathering, they were warned that no one would come. But the first year, close to 100 cowboys and families came and one by one they read their poems.

From the beginning, Hal Cannon explained, the connection of these people to the land was clear. They had often felt wronged by movies and western mythmakers but here they could be proud of their hard work and long days. There was a sense of community among strangers.

Since that first event, people who live on the land have been ravaged by a farm depression that forced many families out of business. And the poetry at the annual gathering now takes on a new seriousness. Workshops have titles like "Ranching culture—will it survive?" and "Ranchers and Environmentalists." The keynote speaker talks about new ways to graze the land. There is an urgency about the future.

Montana rancher and nationally renowned poet Wally McRea writes in four-four square dance cadence of his fears about a West sold to the highest bidder. Wide-open space, he laments in his toe-tapping poem, is vanishing.

Thank the boys for the 'lectric toys
that played the country dance.

Though there's damn little Country left,
pays your money, take yer chance.
The Country Dance ain't got no chance
if mother earth's a whore.
Heel and toe and away we go.
Goin' gone . . . goin' gone . . . goin' gone
There ain't no more.

Espresso

THERE IS NO DENYING that the passion for espresso is sweeping the nation but I always thought cowboy country was safe from this phenomenon. Despite tall tales of camp coffee thick as mud, my husband and I know better. At small-town western cafés, we have gulped down untold cups of watery brew in pursuit of the trace of caffeine lurking in chipped mugs. We know what real cowboys drink. Or we thought we did until the Cowboy Poetry Gathering in Elko, Nevada, last winter.

We saw it as soon as we entered the convention center, smack-dab in the middle of the lobby as big as life and twice as startling—an espresso cart. The polished chrome machine was spewing out hefty cups of java like some volcanic icon to the 1990s under a white awning that boasted "Lattes, Espresso, and Mochas."

Around the room familiar cowboy paraphernalia was prominently displayed. There were neck scarves, chapbooks of poems, music tapes, posters of cowboys on bucking broncs spinning ropes above their heads—the usual friendly reminders of the gathering.

But there was the espresso bar in the middle of everything, and things weren't as they always had been.

Okay, I confess I was one of its best customers. The first morning, I got my drink quickly. There was only one other woman in line. I asked the girl throwing the levers how long the machine had been in place, hoping it was a convention center fixture. But nope. The whole outfit was only several days old, brought in for us. I forked over the exorbitant price for the stout mixture. It was delicious. Cowboys around me were holding the standard paper coffee cup from the snack bar—drinking the safe see-through stuff. But that was the first day.

My next attempt at the espresso bar took five minutes, even with three people working the machine. The second day, there were about ten people when I arrived in the morning. By noon the line extended around the corner, past the poetry session on cowboy humor. Midafternoon, I was sickened at the sight of cowboys lined up clear down the hall past the men's room door and others walking around the hall with foam on their mustaches. I opted for a Pepsi.

For the rest of the weekend I dodged the crowds of wide-brimmed hats and TV cameras, leaving poetry readings in the middle of sessions to get to the espresso cart when the line was the shortest.

On Sunday morning after an unusually late night, my husband and I went by the convention center for a jolt of coffee before the drive home. I was thrilled to see the espresso bar open but soon learned that the machine had given up after its heroic four-day, nonstop effort.

"We've got regular coffee," the woman volunteered and, in response to my question, allowed that it was indeed the "watery stuff" you get around town. "That's the way they like it around here," she added.

The Debate

ON SUNDAY, IN FULL WINTER SUN, my husband and I drove into our ranch headquarters. The animals and ranch hands are in warm southern climates while the livestock are birthing. So the 24 snow-packed miles from town were breathtakingly quiet.

But I felt the need to be there on the land and in the space that has such a hold on me, to walk through my cabin and along the porch, to pull a few brown flower stems from the pots hanging from the eves of the house, to see my garden plot and the tangled raspberry bushes, to chip at a patch of mostly melted ice on a fence post. I had a need to see this place because today it is the subject of controversy, a place in jeopardy, and I am afraid for its future.

Recently Secretary of Interior Bruce Babbitt flew to Idaho to announce his recommendations for grazing fees and the management of livestock on public lands. When I heard why he was coming, my heart stopped for a moment. It was the news we, as livestock producers, feared for some time although none of us could claim to be surprised.

Over the last few years representatives in Congress have proposed higher grazing fees on public lands and then launched hearings around the West. Cattle and sheep producers lined up to testify against the new economic hardship while environmentalists turned out to encourage higher fees to service western lands.

During the 1980s, when I worked with farmers who were being forced off the land, there was blame and fear and broken hopes as families crumbled in one another's arms. Today, we no longer hear the stories of farmers storming local banks or turning guns on themselves. But the struggle still exists. Have coffee at any small-town café and you'll hear about it.

The fear is for our livelihood. Like the timber issue, grazing is a part of the story tearing at the heart of the region. It is the tension between economics and conservation, the conflict between today and tomorrow, the sorrow of weighing tradition against adaptation, and learning how best to care for our families and our land.

And our own ranch operation has been hurt by record-low lamb and cattle prices. My husband and I feared the worst as we went to hear the Secretary unveil his plans.

When he stepped up to the microphone, I held my breath. His first words were gentle. "There must be a place for ranching in the West," he said. "It is often the highest and best use of the land and when families are forced out, ragtag development follows." Then he outlined his plan.

Within a week, voices of the West sounded, shrill and terrifying. Angry friends took the debate to the streets.

Those who understood our connection to the land rallied to "save the West"—our homes and livelihoods—but the events turned political as opposition party lawmakers railed against the administration themselves losing sight of the problem. Others cried out that ranchers are a minority in a dying industry and should get out of the way for the "rest of the West."

There were still others who devised stunts to thrill the media. These people, many of whom I used to call friends, had become strangers. Their wild accusations frightened me. I felt isolated as the sides dug in.

And I wondered, how did we jump over the most important question in the debate? It is not who gets the land but how it is cared for. We all know the treasure of our resources—perhaps no one better than the families who depend on them for their livelihood year in, year out, generation to generation.

Why can't we sit down together and talk about a parcel of land and how to heal it? Why aren't we trying to help one another learn better ways? Why aren't we trying to understand the fears of change?

A week later I went to a panel discussion on the future of ranching at the annual Cowboy Poetry Gathering in Elko, Nevada. The first speaker began, "Polarizing people has never contributed to the discussion and media stunts never provide answers. It's the people who work for real solutions that make things happen."

I listened hard. A rancher from Nevada explained, "We no longer say we're in the cow business. We're in the resource business." She continued, "Who cares who caused what we have today? It doesn't mean we have to have it tomorrow."

These people were talking to my fears. And in their words was a sense of purpose. "The next time you're invited to a meeting to learn how to man the ramparts," one panelist concluded, "skip it. Find a group ready to build a bridge instead."

Shed Lambing

FROM THE EARLIEST DAYS of our sheep operation, our ewes have had their lambs in February and March in sheds along the Snake River. This country is 70 miles to the south of our ranch headquarters and 2,000 feet lower in elevation. Here the icy winds hold the slightest promise of warmth and springtime when it still snows in the north country.

Along the riverbank, activities focused around large, long, canvas-covered sheds where newborn lambs and their mothers were hurriedly brought after the birth to protect them from winter winds.

Several times a day, the herders circled the fields in horse-drawn sleds, feeding the heavy ewes flakes of hay forked onto the crusty snow. They watched each animal closely. After a ewe had her lamb or, even better, twins (which is common), the man called the "drop picker" gathered up the newborn, knowing each ewe would follow her baby inside.

The sheds contained rows of pens, or "jugs," as they're called, made with slats of wood. Once the lamb had stood and sucked and gained strength from its mother, the two would be moved from the small pen to a larger one, often outside, which they shared with other pairs. Then, several days later they'd be moved again to an even larger pen and a larger group of ewes and lambs, and finally to half bands of nearly 500 animals in fenced fields that reached to the river's edge.

We had three sheds, one for the skittish yearling ewes who, birthing for the first time, needed special help. There was a night shed, out of the wind, where the glow from inside would light up the canvas walls "like a lamp-shade," my husband explained. Finally, the east shed by the river was used for the daytime drop.

"When they were really rolling, we'd get 300 lambs a day—sometimes 150 in a night and the same during the day," my husband remembered.

"We'd number the mother and newborn with paint—different colors for each of the six bands and different sides of the body to tell the twins from singles. That way no lamb could get separated from its mother for very long."

The sheds smelled of iodine used to sterilize the umbilical cord and the fresh straw covering the floor of each pen. The men always worked with a sense of urgency. They slept in a bunkhouse with a woodstove, the night men in camps away from the sheds and the cook shack so they could sleep during the day.

For much of the past, and even after I arrived, the herders were Basque, like the cook, Maria. Every day she prepared hearty meals for the crew, filling the long table in the cook shack with bowls of soup, salad, beans, french fries, and lamb stews or roasted chickens and always slices of crusty homemade bread. The men would pass a bota bag of red wine around the table to wash down the food.

The work at the lambing sheds was hard, unpredictable, and round-the-clock as we struggled to save the newborn from the cold. The economics of shed lambing, with its tough work, expensive feed, and huge crews, coupled with plummeting lamb prices nationally, forced us to look for new ways to handle the operation if we were to survive.

In 1984, on the suggestion of a neighbor, we looked south toward warm winter pastures. It was a new idea for us, and soon, as for many other Idaho sheep ranchers, it became a way of life. Eventually, we sold our lambing sheds along the Snake River and now, after only a few years, the old ways seem little more than a whispered memory, a tune heard a long time ago.

Valentine's Day

It is almost Valentine's Day, the day we dazzle those we love. But oh, the pressure to perform as we throw time and money into flowers, candies, and, over the years, an endless succession of candlelight dinners at overpriced restaurants!

My husband used to panic the week before February 14, convinced, and rightfully so, that he could never satisfy my inflated expectations. But several years into our marriage he took me to Las Vegas on Valentine's Day, an experience he has yet to match.

We had been about 90 miles north of that Nevada city. A band of our sheep was pasturing in the flat, lonely Armagosa Valley. It was wild desert country broken only by an occasional abandoned alfalfa field. The community had long since given up hopes of agricultural greatness.

We were expecting more sheep to arrive by truck from Needles, California, two hours south. It was almost dark and four hours late when the vehicle finally appeared at the end of the road. We unloaded the animals into a large pen with water troughs and plenty of space for the ewes and their lambs to pair up. But the dust swirled around the sheep as they ran off the truck, and they lost each other in the dark and in the dust storm they created as they circled the field. We stayed with them until they were quiet.

It was after 8 P.M. when we finally pulled away. We smelled like sheep and were covered with dust, chewing it, blinking it out of our eyes. We drove to the nearest motel in the town of Pahrump 20 miles away, while I grumbled about "a fine way to spend Valentine's Day." To our horror, not only was a familiar motel filled but every bed in town was taken. We had little choice but to drive the next 50 miles to Las Vegas.

An hour later we pulled up to a small motel away from the neon and noise of the Strip. They had no rooms and, worse, they had no luck finding places for other travelers before us. I tried to determine if it was our disheveled appearance that put off the desk clerk or whether things were really grim.

From a lobby phone I dialed, and was turned down at twenty-one locations, from top-of-the-line hotels to skid-row lodgings, all over the city. There was not a room to be had in Las Vegas. The first vacancy I found by phone was two hours south in Needles.

It turned out Valentine's Day was the biggest day of the year in Las Vegas. "People come to get married, don't you know," a desk clerk said. And to make it worse, Friday had been the thirteenth, so it was a hot week-end at the gambling tables. What did we know? We were just there working our sheep.

We drove around aimlessly counting "No Vacancy" signs and finally pulled into a McDonald's, hungry and too dirty and tired to know where else to go. We hadn't eaten since noon.

I got only the top layer of dust washed off my face in the restroom before my husband and I devoured the last burgers they cooked that night. They were dried out around the edges.

Minutes after the McDonald's sign flickered off, we slumped down in the car seats parked in the lot of the first motel we had tried. We were homeless, filthy, and exhausted.

After our Valentine's Day in Las Vegas, my husband and I ask little of each other on February 14. A quiet night at home, a little TV. Life's simple pleasures, nothing more.

Elk

IN OUR WESTERN LANDSCAPE, there are animals everywhere. Sleek antelope, wily coyotes, hardworking beavers, powerful elk. Although they are around us always, some seem more obvious in one season than another. And so it is with the elk during these harsh winter months.

Confused by the deep snows after seven years of drought, they wander the foothills of our ranch in large herds looking for food. Last weekend in town we watched them trail down steep slopes in the heavily populated Sun Valley resort area. It was as if they were deliberately entertaining winter skiers. We joined tourists and locals alike who had pulled off the highway to watch the dignified procession of eighty animals stringing single-file down the hill-side to a haystack. The feed had been put there by Fish and Game employees.

The elk were breathtaking creatures, especially the bulls, one with a six-point, a second with a seven-point, rack. Their horns protruded from huge dark brown heads and they seemed to glide like dancers, regally balancing headdresses as they moved down the muddy trail they'd worn through the deep white snow. They paid no attention to us, even though we were so close we had no need for binoculars.

The elk were victims of change. New housing and escalating development in the resort valley had blocked them from traditional wintering grounds where they once browsed freely along riverbanks on willows and last summer's shoots. Now they depended on ranchers and the Fish and Game for feed in winters as severe as this one.

Later that day we drove into our ranch, stopping to watch a herd of these beautiful animals high on the south side of a mountain ridge. Here the snow had partially melted away, leaving the elk an area to graze. From a distance the ground looked bare but when we stooped to a similar patch of melted snow near the road, we saw small green shoots.

We walked along the trail hard under our feet but not hard enough for the huge weight of elk, and hopped over deep holes where their hooves had broken through the crust. They wandered freely in this winter landscape. We could smell their heavy animal odor in the clear air.

We used binoculars to scan the ridge line and saw more elk warming themselves in the afternoon sun. A few saw us below them and stopped grazing. We stared at each other for a long time, both curious, and somehow connected, even in the distance.

But long shadows began to move in and the air picked up a sudden chill. We turned for the pickup, knowing darkness was close by and that we must leave these magnificent creatures and the silence behind us and find our way back to the warmth of town.

Winter Images

THERE ARE SEVERAL DEEP PURPLE PANSIES by the front door of my mother-in-law's house in Boise. Their petal tips are curled from early-morning frost. Nonetheless they still try to overcome a monthlong tumult of winter.

As often as I yearn for warm weather, especially when I wait for my frosted car to warm in the morning, I remind myself it is only February after all and not time for spring. Then I think back on the roads I've driven recently and remember the beauty found in the images of winter throughout our western landscape.

It came to me first when I saw a cowboy on horseback in a wide empty field along a southern Idaho backroad. It was just after a big snowstorm and the landscape was white. Ice hung off fences. The cowboy sat hunched over on his horse. The collar of his plaid wool jacket was turned up around his neck. He blew on his fingertips. Two dogs hovered at the heels of the horse.

Clearly the man had come ahead to open gates, and now he waited for the other riders pushing a string of Herefords just over the ridge, the animals lifting their heavy legs to get through the knee-deep snow. It was a familiar story. The cowboys were moving the cattle closer to haystacks so feeding them in bad weather would be easier. But in this still life of man, horse and dogs in the white, empty countryside, winter seemed intensely cruel and beautiful at once.

That same morning, I was slowed by a band of sheep, also on the move in the snow. I waved to the owner, a friend, who led the procession from his red truck. Then I began maneuvering my Subaru through the wooly bodies that filled the road. They brushed around the car. Curious white faces peered in at me as we moved by each other. I encouraged them on through the glass between us.

Last week, my husband and I drove directly into the heart of winter. It had only started to snow as we headed out of a small Nevada town, but we soon found ourselves in whiteout conditions and alone on the long stretch of road north to Idaho. The whiteness hung down to the horizon, obscuring distances and leaving us in the loneliness of the close space around our truck. We broke track down the highway.

In Wildhorse Canyon, willows shot up from the ground, red and orange against the whiteness. Bare trees followed creeks, and the water was covered with snow so that streams seemed mere indentations in the landscape. Cedar trees hung like lace cones from slopes that squeezed the road. Red rock stood in defiant shapes around us as we skimmed through the hushed landscape.

Then the country opened up. Cattle, five across, strung out along a fence line for a quarter mile. The procession struggled forward in the deep snow; the animals' brown backs were dusted white. Farther along, more cattle huddled in the willows. "They search for the shelter of willows when it snows," my husband observed.

The drive was filled with whiteness and silence and scenes of the commitment it takes to survive on the land. And in the stark beauty of this season, the images charge the imagination, leaving me reluctant to abandon these winterscapes for spring too soon.

Gray Ranch

THE GRAY RANCH, south of Animas, New Mexico, occupies over 326,000 acres of open grass valleys interrupted here and there by mountains and low hills. It stretches south to Mexico and west to the Peloncillo Mountains at the Arizona border. It is rough country but beautiful in its primitive rock and low brush landscape.

My husband and I stayed a night at the Gray Ranch. In a half-day drive with its manager the next morning, we covered only a portion of this sprawling ranch land. But we came away with a strong sense of its history shaped by border activity with Mexico. Names filled in the details: Pancho Villa, General Pershing, Outlaw and Smuggler Mountains, Chinaman Hills. We drove up the historic San Luis Pass, which straddles the Continental Divide. Its hillsides were covered with cholla cactus, a sign the area had been used hard in the past rustling cattle back and forth across the Mexican border.

In the morning stillness, the stories might have seemed like folklore if it weren't for the occasional glint of sunlight thrown off passing vehicles along Mexico Highway 2 at the end of the valley.

The Gray Ranch has a long and rich history but its current story may be the most interesting. In 1990 it was purchased by The Nature Conservancy to preserve its undisturbed space and unique indigenous grassland. Soon after, local ranchers learned that the U.S. Fish and Wildlife Service was interested in the ranch as a recreation area that might attract as many as 65,000 people a year.

This brought community people together, who feared their fate might resemble the ravages of Tucson and the sprawling development of much of southern Arizona. They formed the Malpai Borderlands Group to protect the land and its ecosystem and to maintain their livelihood as ranchers.

They began talking to people they had thought were adversaries, the Forest Service, Bureau of Land Management, and environmentalists, only to discover they shared the same goals for the region. A rancher, a member of the group, decided to buy the Gray Ranch with family funds and set up a foundation.

They were neighbors, Wendy and Warner Glenn said in the first newsletter for the group. They had worked together to get telephones, school bus service, and rural electricity. Now it was time to tackle their biggest challenge, saving the land.

The Gray Ranch became their showpiece and staging area. They initiated two programs. The first encouraged the return of healthy grasses through controlled fire. This replaced years of fire-suppression policies that allowed scrub brush to take over the landscape.

Second, they began grass banking to provide grazing lands for ranchers who needed to rest their own dry or overused pastures. In exchange, a rancher paid a grazing fee and turned over a conservation easement to the Malpai Group, securing the area from developers.

What I like best about the story is neighbors working as a community to save their lands when as individuals they might not be able to do so. And they are defending their livelihood without the acrimony that has defined so much of the western debate.

The Malpai Borderlands members say they are the "radical center." I like that idea. As others line up on the extremes, I feel at home with the ideas of these families, and the center seems a little less lonely today because of them.

Las Vegas Retro

SEVERAL WEEKS BEFORE WE ARRIVED IN LAS VEGAS, I made a hotel reservation. Just a precaution. After all, the last time my husband and I were in that city together, every hotel room was filled and we slept in the car. It was Valentine's Day and I promised myself this would never happen again.

It took a long day of driving the length of Nevada over isolated roads to get to this remarkable city, but I was determined that my husband see the place on the way to our sheep camps. "You won't believe it," I predicted, for it had been almost ten years since he had been there. I had attended a meeting in January and was shocked at the new Las Vegas.

My husband and I arrived at dusk. All the neon on the south end of town, the original casino area, was in full blaze. But as we approached the main part of "the Strip," now a sort of giant theme park, there was less glitz. Instead these hotels were spotlighted rather like the Lincoln or Jefferson Memorial in Washington, D.C.—vastly more imposing and here, pretentious.

I pointed out the sights as we drove. "There's the Eiffel Tower," I announced. "And the Grand Canal, the lakes of northern Italy, the Statue of Liberty, the New York Skyline, the MGM Lion, the Pyramids and Sphynx of Egypt." In a 2-mile stretch, we had practically circled the globe. Amazing. And almost so real.

But it was the slight tinge of fake that threw us off. Not to mention the enormity of each casino hotel. And I was left wondering how this came to be, especially after we pulled back the curtains in our room and found ourselves staring at the Eiffel Tower. This certainly beat sleeping in the car.

At my January meeting I had been stunned by these changes in Las Vegas. Our luncheon speaker, a dynamic history professor at the University of Nevada–Las Vegas, regaled us with the story of the new city. "This town has gone from a Mafia-run operation to a corporate-owned, Wall

Street–financed spectacle," he explained. "We've moved from gambling to tourism to entertainment. And we can give you anything you want." As if for my benefit he added, "There are 120,000 hotel rooms today in Las Vegas. Twice the 60,000 rooms in all of New York City."

It was staggering. Later I roamed hotels with friends and found not just slots and gambling tables but the finest shopping—Tiffany; Cartier; Gucci; art galleries with original Picassos, Monets, Renoirs; and eateries with an array of gourmet creations from the best chefs in the country.

Clearly, as casino gambling spreads into communities around the U.S. and middle-class Americans begin to make a quick thousand in the stock market on a regular basis, Las Vegas has had to retool itself.

Today it is the fastest growing city in the West, with housing sprawl miles into the desert to prove it. It is the American Dream for its thousands of workers who have unionized (it is today the largest union town in the West), bought homes, and are sending their kids to college.

But for all of this, my husband and I are reminded as we wander the huge hotels, it is still almost elegant, almost the experience of a lifetime. Despite the changes, it is still Las Vegas, a city of dreams and dreamers.

Night at the Ranch

IT IS SPRING ALMOST EVERYWHERE in southern Idaho and my husband and I are struck with a longing to go home. We knew from an attempt to drive the road a week earlier that winter had not released its grasp on our country. We would have to ski to get into our ranch. So we decided that if we were going to tackle the silent backcountry, we would stay for the night.

We threw cross-country skis in the car and packs loaded with water, bread, cheese, fruit, soup packets, coffee, an extra T-shirt, and a toothbrush and headed the pickup north from Carey.

When the pavement ended, the truck spun into thick tracks of mud. We followed the road north in four-wheel-drive as snow patches and slick ground swung us from side to side. Finally there was nothing ahead but fields of snow.

We parked and then loaded ourselves and Jock, our black-and-white Border collie, with packs, clamped on skis, and headed off across a neighbor's field toward the ranch. Going home.

It was full sunshine and brilliant blue sky. My husband and I glided easily across the whiteness still so deep we saw only the tips of posts as we slid over the top of barbed-wire fences. Our dog ran along deliriously beside us.

I was beginning to slow down as we passed through the white gate to our ranch. "Only two more miles, two cattle guards, and three fields," I thought, and remembered the night several summers ago when I had gotten a flat tire at sunset just outside the gate. I decided I could walk home more easily than I could change a tire in the thin evening light. But after I started out, I thought I'd never see the cattle guard and the end of the first field. Now on skis, I was pacing off the distance again.

By the time the ranch buildings appeared on the horizon, the sun was weakening. Despite the lateness, I slowed down to absorb the familiar landscape. Each silent place stirred memories of summer activity.

I looked hard to see the road into my mother-in-law's house but I made out only the slightest furrow in the snow. I peered through bare cottonwood branches at the bunkhouses usually hidden from the road. Four wooden sleighs were lined up silently bearing the full weight of winter's snow. I skied across the bridge, stopping to stare at the rushing water. The red barn, outbuildings, and corrals stood out boldly in the whiteness.

I followed my husband's thin tracks to our cabin. His skis stood like sentries by the gate. I set mine next to his, climbed over the wooden slats, and sank into thigh-high snow. Thinking better of this, I picked out my husband's deep footprints and followed them to the front door.

Despite the chill in the kitchen, the lights made it seem inviting. My husband was starting a fire in the large, black Majestic-brand cookstove. I filled up several kettles with snow that we would melt for washing and heard him chopping more wood to get us through the night. The sky was streaked with color. It was not quick to give up on this day.

The large woodstove warmed the kitchen quickly but our bedroom took longer with only a small wall heater at work. As darkness closed in around us, we settled in by the fire for some dinner. There was a gentle silence around us broken only by an occasional popping log in the stove, and after a time, the thud of melting snow sliding from the roof to the ground below.

But it was the next morning I had been waiting for—to open my eyes to the vast space outside my bedroom window. The sky was still pale from the night. A single brown stem from a forgotten summer flower shuddered slightly in the window box outside the glass. I watched the light move across the landscape, filling in shadows. I did not want to leave.

In the kitchen, my husband was putting wood on the fire. We made coffee and toasted bread. The day brightened steadily.

Reluctantly we retraced our steps out of the cabin, climbing the gate and putting on skis again. We stopped more often on the trip out, memorizing sights and sounds to take with us.

Back in the truck, we scanned the horizon, looking at snow contours on hillsides that would feed springs for summer. We looked for running water, signs we would soon return.

But for now we settled into the thought that we had been a part of the silence and solitude that are the gift of winter to this landscape. The time when the earth quiets, sleeps, and heals itself in the hush.

The Cattle

I FIRST SAW FLAT TOP SHEEP COMPANY RANCH in winter with its owner. The landscape was covered with snow as we passed willows and lanky cottonwood trees without leaves. My friend pointed out draws and ridges where cattle roamed in summer, and we pulled up to watch black cows eating hay looped across white fields of snow. And I remember in the intense stillness thinking that the cows looked natural in this setting, which seemed like a sharply focused black-and-white photograph.

That summer I made a business of learning more about the cattle. I liked the looks of the Angus, different from the jowly Herefords with their pink-rimmed eyes that I knew from other western landscapes. My friend explained that he raised a long-bodied Angus that produced top-quality beef. "Our first Angus had stocky bodies and shorter legs," he explained. "These are much better."

I soon realized that it all came down to the bulls. A brown Swiss who mated with an Angus cow gave us a dark brown offspring. These calves grew into good mothers that produced a large supply of milk for their young.

For a time we had Charolais bulls, the powerful, creamy-white French breed that allowed us to raise a bigger calf. One that also produced a white calf, a startling and exotic sight when the first dropped from its black mother. Confused cows came from around the field to surround this white bundle. They licked it, pushed it with their heads, smelled it, and bellowed at its strangeness. It took five or six births for the cows to calm down, but who knows if the confused mothers ever fully understood this turn of events.

This bull business has taken my husband and me to a lot of sales in a lot of auction barns. At one, we wandered over to a pen of Brangus bulls. They were all the rage at the time but I could not understand the interest in this animal with long, drooping ears that seemed to pull its head into a thin teardrop shape. We stuck to our Angus.

And we've visited a number of breeding ranches, like the one owned by E. G. Foote, where recently we walked through brown fields tinted the palest spring green. The Foote ranch sits along the wide benchland next to the Snake River in Owyhee County.

This day, my husband and I followed E. G. into his fieldstone office building, its entry hall and reception room lined with trophy cases. Crowding the walls were pictures of family gathered around one prize animal or another, everyone, including the black bulls, beaming for the camera.

My husband sat at E. G.'s desk studying a small chart with statistics on each animal. In the hall, E. G. explained his product to me.

"It's not the animal's weight or fat," he told me, "but the marbling in the carcass that earns top choice or prime grade for a calf. That's what we strive for, the best meat possible."

He pointed to pictures of animals from champion bulls called Scotch Cap, Paramount Ambush, New Trend 315, tracking winners like Bear Tooth Ice and Traveler. I wondered who came up with these names and wished I had a flowchart for the brothers, sisters, and offspring sired by these prized bulls as the lineages, like the pictures on the wall, circled around and around.

E. G.'s family, parents, and grandparents have been in the breeding business for forty-five years, twenty-one of them run by E. G. at this ranch in Idaho. Although he raises some livestock for meat, he is mostly in the business of producing breeding animals. And E. G. has earned his reputation showing and winning with his bulls around the West. The ribbons in the trophy cases read like a road map of the region: the Calgary Stampede, the Pacific National Exhibition in Vancouver, the California State Fair.

We left the office to wander through the pens that held the range of his stock, from four small yearling bulls to the hulking form of his prized show bull called Footes Traveler. We climbed over the white wood fence into a lot with thirty full-sized Angus from which we would select six.

My husband had already noted several animals on his work sheet for their pelvic size. These will breed a line of cows that calve easily. I looked for bulls with broad backs, which E. G. told me was a sign of the best rib eye. "The back is where you want the size, not in fat."

It didn't take long to choose the animals we wanted. They stood out to us in the roving group of males and my husband and I wrote down their ear-tag numbers, checking with each other as we selected.

It is like this at each breeding ranch we visit. We climb fences to wander through muddy pens, circling around and around skittish animals to fully inspect prospective parents.

"It is a long-term investment, like planting a tree," my husband will always say, as he did the day we pulled away from the Foote ranch. "The traits in the bulls we chose today will develop mother cows and determine the quality of our herd for generations."

On each occasion I let his sense of pride settle over me after we've agreed on price and delivery dates with the producer. There is the satisfaction of business accomplished.

And at these times I think about my first glimpse of Black Angus against white snow in midwinter, remembering how at home they looked on the ranch meadows. And I know that I saw that landscape and my life differently after that day.

Heifers

WE DRIVE INTO OUR WINTER RANCH HEADQUARTERS at Kimama on the edge of southern Idaho farm country. To the north is sagebrush and lava rock desert. It is Sunday morning and we are going to meet our grown son and head cowboy to sort out heifers.

The flat, open countryside is white as far as the eye can see. We turn off the main highway onto snow-packed roads and drive between white berms piled higher than the pickup.

"What do ya think?" I ask my husband.

"At least 10 feet," he answers. I whistle, impressed. It is the winter we've been waiting for after years of drought.

Five miles in, we pass the row of sturdy spruce, a landmark in this empty landscape. The trees are still young but already this winter they have been a lifesaving windbreak, keeping fiercely blowing snows off cattle in the large pens behind them.

We pull past the shop, barn, and corrals to the farmhouse. To the north are two more pens where the heifers mill around as if expecting us. We will separate them for their first spring breeding.

I pull on high boots, a hat, and warm gloves and follow the men into the deep snows. Walking turns into hard work as we struggle across the field, sinking every few steps through a white crust into soft, thigh-high powder.

But the sorting alley is clear of snow and the 250 heifers move easily through the line as the men sort them by color and size. In the first run we divide the pure Angus from those born from a brown Swiss cow. The latter are slightly lighter in color. The second time through, we sort the large from the small heifers. All but these small ones will be bred to Angus bulls.

I stand on a mound of snow so high I am even with the top fence post, and from that vantage point I can see for miles on this clear, blue day.

Several hours later, fingers and toes stinging from the cold, we head into the house where our cowboy's wife has fixed bowls of stew for us. There is homemade bread still warm from the oven. I look out the window at the silent whiteness and wish I could stay. But it will be spring before we move back to our cabin by the creek 70 miles to the north. For now I'll just content myself with this Sunday afternoon in thigh-high snows at our high-desert winter headquarters at Kimama.

Kimama

THE TOWNSITE OF KIMAMA is no more than a spot on the map, a few trees, a water tower outlined against the sky, a whispered presence of the small railroad stop where early in the twentieth century steam engines drew water. The tower is one of the last left standing in the United States.

Kimama is easy to miss along rural Highway 24, the road that runs east from the town of Shoshone through the high desert and past grain fields with large irrigation pivots, ending 45 miles later in the town of Minidoka. Kimama is maybe halfway between. There, buried in desert brush and tall crested wheat near the water tower, you can still pick out the abandoned townsite and the old tracks from the horse-and-wagon road to American Falls.

And you see the few farms at the edge of the desert, the jumping-off landscape beyond the heavily cultivated communities of Rupert, Burley, and Paul. These farming areas stretched themselves this far, then gave up.

Probably because at Kimama things are no longer easy. Here the lava rock becomes too dense to clear for the plow. Here rocks turn to boulders and boulders become ridges and wildness takes over.

But this is where we have set up our winter headquarters. On a butte at the edge of the desert, my husband moved a house for our head cowboy. There is a shop, corrals, pens for the livestock, and a tack room. I often think this is where my husband would live if the house were not already filled with family.

For several years we wintered our steers and bulls here while our cows were in California. But change caught up with us and now our cows also stay home, grazing on Kimama pastures and on snowy days feeding at mangers in large pens near the house. And although we have always raised hay and grain each summer on fields around the house, now we raise more than ever to get our animals through the winter.

So with this change there is new activity at our farm on the edge of the desert. And new reasons for my husband to spend his days here checking the livestock, knocking ice off the water troughs, and measuring the feed.

He is in his element because Kimama is his favorite country. When I ask him why, he tells me that from a rancher's perspective the grasses are unbeatable. They are green early in the spring when much of the rest of Idaho is still under snow. And it's the cost of feeding animals in the winter that can bury an operation.

But it's more than that, he'll add. It's the space in every direction. The sweeping view of mountains to the south and north and the 70 miles in between of wild lava rock landscape. The patterns of light always change the look of this desert.

There are no buildings, little evidence of people. And in this setting, my husband explains, there is the strongest sense of the cycles of our lives. The seasons start here with the birth of the calves, the greening of grasses. And from Kimama he can look north to the mountains and our ranch headquarters, and imagine all the possibilities of spring and summer ahead.

Ranch Women

THE DEBATE IN THE WEST reached into new areas for me last week when I was invited to speak at a regional Forest Service training program in Oregon. "Our agenda's heavy on the white male ranch culture," the organizer told me on the phone. "We want to hear from women who live on the land and write about the West." How could I resist?

For a month, twelve Forest Service managers from the Northwest had been studying together. They had toured Idaho farms, ranches, and sale barns. They walked through pastures, watched ewes lamb and cows calve in midwinter muddy fields. They listened to the stories of ranch families living on the land in a program called "Hides, Hooves, Horns, and Heartaches." The experience was an attempt by that federal agency to help its employees better understand what lies behind the conflicts over public lands.

What they heard were new words for familiar fears. The same fears and anger of families from timber-dependent communities now translated into the ranching vernacular. These managers told me they felt caught between angry factions of resource users and environmentalists as if they were the enemy for people looking for someone to blame.

First understand the panic, I advised. Look behind the violent words at the fear. Instead of threatening ranchers, work with them, help them see how they should manage the land differently. Encourage experiences like those of rancher Doc Hatfield in central Oregon, who opened his home to environmentalists, government land managers, and neighboring livestock producers. They discussed a plan for the land.

"I'll do it," he said. "Just let me run my cattle and I'll meet your conditions." And he has—transforming meadows and riparian areas into model environmental landscapes.

There was a young Forest Service manager who grew up in an Oregon logging and ranching family. Now, she told me, she felt helpless, unable to bring warring factions together. Recently a favorite uncle tried to calm her. "Sometimes you've just got to leave people where they're at," he said.

We talked all morning as we toured a local farm, and during lunch hour, which, I had been warned, was an "unusual" one. But somehow, sitting down to a meal of tongue, sweetbreads, and liver seemed almost natural if I were to talk about the role of ranch women in the West. After all, wasn't this what people ate when they could not afford to let anything on a slaughtered animal go to waste? And when I asked one of the local women who brought the food and if she ate like this at home, she laughed. "Let's just say my son always asked for steak on his birthday," she replied.

After the meal, it was my turn to speak. I talked about women on the land and their connection to nature, to family, and to ranch life, explaining that those of us writing today are filling in the landscape for those who don't know this place. We are telling the stories for those who don't have the words. We are writing about doctoring, riding, rounding up livestock, cooking, tending kids, and now, working at Wal-Mart 90 miles down the road to pay bills the ranch can't cover.

We are writing because we are frightened for the future of this place and we are writing to remember it even as it is changing. Some women of the West are writing of the detail of daily lives. They are the chroniclers. Some are writing lyrically, releasing through their words the soul of this landscape. They are the poets. And some are writing urgently of the war between fear and hope among western people. They are our political conscience.

Women of the West are writing today about this land as few others are, and we are writing because we must.

Love Letter

TODAY IT IS SPRING and the soft air brushes over me, bringing with it hope and anticipation. Its warmth will melt the last snows at our ranch head-quarters—elevation 6,000 feet—and we will go home, abandoning our nomadic winter ways.

The livestock will follow, most coming by truck from California pastures where they have grazed and borne their young. I imagine they are as anxious as we are to return to the green foothills of the Pioneer Mountains, to wet lands full of promise after punishing years of drought. I realize that I long to see our rivers and creeks rush full and fast through tangles of willows and between towering stands of cottonwoods only now just beginning to unfold small leaves down long branches.

On the meadows, there will be antelope and deer with their young. The sandhill cranes will arrive to nest and give birth. The horses will foal.

Here in this environment, this place where life and death are so intricately woven together, and now in this season of second chances, I am full of hope. And I remember the first letter I ever received from my husband, years before we were to marry. It was early spring.

We didn't know each other well, but I knew he was convinced we should spend more time together. I was not as certain and yet I was intrigued by this man of the land and his faraway Idaho ranch. The day his letter came, I put it aside, afraid of its urgent demands. Later, when I read the pages, I was startled.

He spoke only of his ranch. Of his first trip for the year into the back-country, of snowmelt rushing along the road, of green grasses on south slopes of hillsides, of antelope running free, of a lone buck close to the road.

He wrote that he had pulled up near the animal and that the two seemed to study the landscape together in the warm spring sunshine, each absorbed in the silence, in the space. It was as if the buck knew he was home at last, my friend wrote me.

And in this simple sentence, I understood this man's longings and his love. It was a love letter from him but not the message I had anticipated. That evening, sitting far away reading and rereading the story of man and buck at home at last, I knew I held a love letter that would change my life forever.

About the Author

DIANE JOSEPHY PEAVEY grew up on the East Coast and spent many childhood summers driving across the West to a second home in Joseph, Oregon, with her family and father, renowned historian Alvin Josephy, Jr. These trips gave her an early rooted connection to the people and the wide-open spaces of the West. For the past twenty years she has lived with her husband, John Peavey, at the Flat Top Sheep Company ranch in south central Idaho.

Diane Josephy Peavey is passionately involved in activities related to her chosen home. She has served on the board of directors for High Country News and the Idaho Nature Conservancy and is former literature director for the Idaho Commission of the Arts. She is also the founder and coordinator of the Trailing of the Sheep Festival, a folklife fair and parade that celebrates the people, traditions, and history of the sheep industry in the United States—an example of how the old and new West can coexist.

In addition to ranching with her husband and family, Peavey has been a radio essayist for Idaho Public Radio since 1991, telling stories of a western landscape that is fragile, uncompromising, and rife with controversies. Her work has appeared in numerous magazines and journals, including *Boise* magazine, *Range* magazine, *Talking River Review*, and *Northern Lights*. She has also contributed to the anthologies *Woven on the Wind, Written on Water, Shadow Cat,* and *Where the Morning Light's Still Blue. Bitterbrush Country* is her first book.